DAVID HUN
Marlborough
the army) at C
English and F
Judy in India.
England, Rhodesia and India and has lectured in
Europe, Africa, India and the USA. His last post was that of Registrar of
Haileybury. He has performed poetry in many locations, including Indian
fort-palaces, British embassies and cruise ships. After retirement he and
Judy worked with GAP in India. They have three children and four grand-
children and now live in the Lake District.

INKLINGS

*How imperfectly we express the little
that we DO know! Nevertheless,
the ink still flows!*

To Judy,
who has lived with my muse
for fifty one years

This edition first published in 2018 by David A. E. Hunt.
Published in Great Britain by Horse & Farrier Barn Productions,
Newton-in-Cartmel, Grange-Over-Sands, Cumbria, LA11 6JQ.
Printed and bound by
CPI Group (UK) Ltd, Croydon, CR0 4YY

Designed and typeset by Justin Hunt © 2018
justinaehunt@gmail.com

A CIP catalogue record for this book is available from the British Library.

ISBN-13: 978-1-5272-1723-2

❖

INKLINGS

A MEDLEY OF POEMS

BY

DAVID A. E. HUNT

Designed by
Justin Hunt

INDEX

☞ FOREWORD

'Boundless is the map a poet charts' writes David Hunt – and few poets illustrate the truth of this aphorism better than he. He covers an extraordinary range of topics with intelligence, zest and a delightful sense of self-deprecating humour. His precise powers of observation are reminiscent of the comedian Michael McIntyre and his broad education peeps out from behind an array of literary and erudite allusions.

He is also accessible, refusing to take cover behind incomprehensible 'cleverness'. John Betjeman meets R.S.Thomas in many of his poems, which can be deeply moving as well as laugh-loud funny. One of the most entertaining sections of this slim volume is entitled 'Things they say': a wry look at some of the expressions in common currency, which will appeal especially to readers of Lyn Truss's 'Eats Shoots and Leaves'. But there is also much here about awe, as we are transported to Cornwall, Cumbria and the Himalayas. And he reflects gracefully on themes which affect us all – from the ageing process to the way in which we use our time here on earth.

David Hunt is a talented musician as well as a gifted poet and I love the rhythm as much as the rhyming in his work. I showed these poems to a friend, a headmaster and English specialist, who had no hesitation in awarding them a straight alpha, with a variety of comments – from 'clear, lucid, crisp and immediate (like Orwell's prose)' to 'unpretentious and unselfconscious'. Hunt's vivid imagery ("the gossamer coy négligée of Spring") and mastery of language make him a delight to read, while the variety of styles he employs means that there is something here for everyone. His own love of poetry is obvious in the way he writes: his faith lends insight and sensitive awareness – and the illustrations subtly enhance the text.

This book is a gem. So (to quote the poem) – 'Enjoy!'

James Newcome, Bishop of Carlisle
National Chaplain to the Royal British Legion

☞ INTRODUCTION

Great poetry is truth-bearing. Seamus Heaney said that poetry "offers a clarification, a fleeting glimpse of a potential order of things beyond confusion". I found this in the excitement of discovering, at school, Milton's 'Paradise Lost' and Coleridge's 'Ancient Mariner'. At that stage I started to write my own and (cheekily, as a 14-year-old) sent my poems to the Poet Laureate John Masefield. He generously replied – a handwritten letter (in which he made no comment on my verses!) giving me all sorts of practical tips. I revere his memory.

My poetry makes no claim to greatness – though much of it comes from the heart. Some of these poems are concerned with trivia – such as the platitudes of everyday conversation and the irritating clichés we all fall back on. Others are a direct response to some insight or experience that has left its mark (like Wordsworth's 'spontaneous overflow of powerful feelings... recollected in tranquillity'). Some are observations on life and fellow human beings, some are soppily nostalgic. Some are an expression of the Christian faith and tradition in which I was reared (faltering though my own faith may often be).

I confess to being a compulsive versifier. I write a poem most days – usually before breakfast. (Judy's spirits must sink when she sees yet another offering next to the cornflakes.) Absolutely anything can spark off a poem – including requests from friends for verses to mark a special occasion. Quantity does not, of course, mean quality! I can only fall back on the words of Shakespeare's Touchstone, "an ill-favoured thing, sir, but my own". I can also echo the playwright Tom Stoppard, who said: "Every time I blink there's a play begging to be written...There is so much to write about, it's like having *nothing* to write about!" Fortunately much is made possible by the vast riches of our wonderful language.

I am hugely grateful to my son Justin, who has energetically pursued this book's publication and skillfully designed it; to Bishop James Newcome, for his encouragement and for the stimulus of his small poetry-reading group; to the many friends who have urged me to publish; and most of all to my wife Judy, without whose longsuffering support this book would never have come about.

Newton-in-Cartmel, Cumbria

ON WRITING A POEM

T.S.Eliot describes some lines in 'The Four Quartets' as:
 "...not very satisfactory,
 A periphrastic study in a worn-out poetical fashion,
 Leaving one still with the intolerable wrestle
 With words and meanings."   (East Coker, 68)

Compose a poem only when you have to!
Write when the words come hammering at your door!
Speak of those aspirations that you hold to -
Which, brought to bed, leave womb enough for more.

A poem should not stand on ceremony,
Does not pretend, sings what it feels and sees,
To truth it bears elusive testimony.
Too deep to plumb, a poem yet can please.

When all is said, a poem remains unfinished:
More than the sum, it is, of all its parts.
Completeness leaves a poem defined, diminished –
While boundless is the map a poet charts.

A poem has ideas above its station,
For always there will stubbornly remain
Some fleeting figment of imagination,
Some truant thing you strove, and failed, to name -
Though it was worth the striving, all the same.

July 2016

POETS ARE THE TRUMPETS WHICH SING TO BATTLE · POETS ARE THE UNACKNOWLEDGED LEGISLATORS OF THE WORLD. SHELLEY

1

FANCIES

❖

NATURE'S WARDROBE

The unabashed stark nudity of Winter,
The gossamer coy négligée of Spring,
The magisterial full fig of high Summer
To whose rich tatters Autumn seeks to cling –
'Til Winter once again bares everything.

June 2015

A winter walk up to the Damn above High Newton, Cumbria.

WINTER

Fallen is the summer's splendour,
    All his garb in disarray,
Prey to winter's bleak agenda –
    Gone the zest of yesterday.

Nothing can restore earth's glory
    Nor its nakedness disguise
Nor sweeten winter's soulful story -
    Nothing can make the sap to rise.

Crepuscular the winter's dawning,
    Drear the breaking of the day,
Desultory and chill the morning,
    Brief the pale sun's fitful stay.

And yet - for all this barren-seeming
    Brick-hard world so stultified,
Beneath our feet the earth is teeming,
On the horizon light is gleaming,
Within us stirs the spirit - scheming
    For Spring and Eastertide!

August 2016

DANDELION

Though its English name is derived from the French 'dent de lion'
('lion's tooth'), in France the dandelion is called 'pissenlit'.

Proud dandelion, running riot along the banks and borders,
    Yellow and unabashed you flaunt your seed,
A herbal medicine said to be a cure for dread disorders –
    And yet a garish, pestilential weed.

And some have named you "Cankerwort" or "Blow-ball"
                    or "Swine's Snout"
    And other designations unaesthetic:
In France you are a "Piss-in-bed" – for there is little doubt
    The dandelion's a potent diuretic.

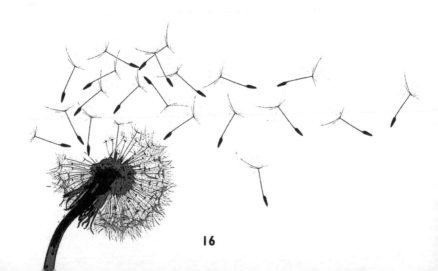

Men see you as the scourge of lawns, allotments, flower-beds,
 And out of crazy paving you will grow.
But children love you for your "clock", which – puffed at –
                                        gently sheds
 A little drifting cloud of seedy snow.

While daisies are more dainty-sweet and primroses more mellow
 And willow-herbs more stately dignified,
While pansies prink and violets shrink before your brazen bellow,
You – bold as brass – spring from the grass, defiantly bright yellow –
 The Lion's Teeth are bared in all their pride.

May 2015 ✍

LAMBS IN OUR FIELD

O blithe newcomer to our field
   Beyond the kitchen sink,
Now Cartmel Easter bells have pealed,
   Rejoicing at Spring's brink -
Your newborn leggy life revealed
   At every jump and jink..

I dry the dishes, see you bound,
   On springs your little feet,
'Til drawn to that protective sound,
   The strong maternal bleat;
Deaf to distractions, comfort found,
   You tug at your mother's teat.

Beyond you, all the ancient beauty
   Of a Cumbrian fell;
Around you, chiming Heaven's bounty,
   Every Cartmel bell.
And He that made music and mountain
   Made you, sweet lamb, as well.

April 2015

BIRDS

Heaven's emissaries, what message do you bring?
Heaven's choristers, what anthems do you sing?
Heaven's jewellers, what are those pearls you string?
Heaven's denizens forever on the wing -
Heavens alive – enshrining everything!

February 2016

Temptation of Adam and Eve. Genesis - after Raphael.

FORBIDDEN

'He was a true poet and of the Devil's party without knowing it.'
(William H. Marshall, about Milton and 'Paradise Lost')

"Of man's first disobedience and the fruit
Of that forbidden tree..." Thus the blind bard,
To justify God's ways and so refute
Man's arguments, wrote much – but dropped his guard.
Of Satan's party, he! That clever snake
Ran coils round Eve and flattered to entice;
Beguiling her with reasonings opaque
To tempt her man, he wrecked their Paradise -..
And in the process managed to disarm
God-fearing Milton, making fullest use
Of all his sophistries and devilish charm:
And lo! the poet himself he did seduce!

From this, it cannot be denied or hidden:
The best may fall for that which is forbidden!

December 2010 ✍

GRACE

Grace is a lovely word. It long since came
To speak of things that lull and charm and please:
Wild geese in flight – a flowing, shimmering skein –
And ballerinas, swans and willow trees,

An Indian girl in sari, with a jar
Balanced indifferently upon her head -
A natural grace, more beautiful by far
Than any on the catwalk carefully bred.

A grace-note is an ornament indeed
(The melody without it remains whole)
Whereof the harmony has no great need:
It yet hints at the beauty of the soul.

Thus we may find in plain and artless face
- Beyond mere pulchritude - amazing Grace!

September 2015 ✍

A Rajasthani women

THE SPORTED OAK

To "sport one's oak" is an ancient Cambridge custom signifying that one is 'not at home' to visitors by closing the oak (or outer) door of one's rooms.

When we as students lived within the College
    Our outer door would serve us as a cloak
For dissipation, or pursuit of knowledge,
    Or sleep indeed – we'd simply sport our oak!

A sported oak dissuaded friends from trying,
    Its message (true or false): "I am not here".
Though sported oaks might be accused of lying,
    Our plea for space was patently sincere.

To such sure means of privacy I resorted,
    Safely immured with crib and library tome
And lecture notes, my oak being firmly sported,
    Telling the world that I was "not at home".

Some share their lives – unbelted, open-hearted,
    Always with space and time for other folk.
But some there are whose sharing never started –
    The hidden ones, who always sport their oak.

And there are oaks that always will be sported,
    Shutting us out from what goes on inside.
Yet no sincere approach was ever thwarted
    By those (thank God!) whose doors stay open wide.

March 2006   *First Court, Christ's College*

PHILTRUM

Only very recently did I discover the name of the little, unregarded groove below the nose – and it is not in my dictionary. A poem is called for!

Of all the features of a face, the ones that all men own,
The names and shapes are plain to see, their uses are
> well known:
>> The nose, of course, and mouth and chin
>> And eyes and ears and cheeky grin
>> And cheekbones just below the skin
>> And dimples, wrinkles – all thrown in –
On every face they're shown.

But of the features we possess, and right across the spectrum,
There's one that's never talked about – it's just below the septum:
>> The 'nose-thirls' (nostrils) mark the place
>> (A hair- lip else would fill the space),
>> From nose to upper lip we trace
>> A little groove upon the face –
The feature called a PHILTRUM

"Philtrum" comes from Greek and speaks of amorous devotion
(A philtre is, as all men know, a powerful love potion).
>> Behind moustaches they may hide,
>> But PHILTRA cannot be denied,
>> Un-named, perhaps, but found worldwide,
>> Beguiling grooves, a source of pride -
>> But what they're for (we must confide)
We really have no notion.

April 2012   *Royal Doulton Toby Jug*

ATHALIE

Racine's 'Athalie' traces the Old Testament story of Athaliah, the ruthless and idolatrous Queen of Judah, who in a nightmare is visited by her dead mother, Jezebel – a portent of her own bloody end. This poem was inspired by a single line.

"C'était pendant l'horreur d'une profonde nuit"
    The alexandrine verse leaps from the page:
Sleep-haunted Queen of Judah, the inglorious Athalie,
    Sees her demise, its pity and its rage.

The horrors of that most horrendous, friendless, endless night!
    The inspissated gloom of the abyss!
Proud Queen, your crimes unspeakable are surely brought
                                  to light,
Your mother comes, her ravaged features hideously bedight –
    Dread Jezebel, your bitter nemesis.

Thus, at the nadir of the night, appeared
    The tattered, bloody, mire-bedraggled she;
The dogs fought over her, while devils fleered
    At Baal-loving, baleful Athalie.
"C'était pendant l'horreur d'une profonde nuit."

July 2015 ✍

Athaliah

Athaliah (/ˌæθəˈlaɪ.ə/; Hebrew: עֲתַלְיָה, ʻĂtalyâ; "God is exalted"; Greek: Γοθολία; Latin: Athalia) was queen consort of Judah as the wife of King Jehoram, a descendant of King David, and later queen regnant c.841–835 BCE.

ODE TO MY PIANO

I have loved you a long time.
Always you have occupied a hallowed corner of the house,
custodian of hidden power, an object of distracting beauty.
I have loved the black-and-whiteness of your keyboard,
 bared for embrace,
The satinwood softness of your skin, the undeniable curves
 of your frame,
The expectancy of your lifted lid, poised to proclaim.

And then,...
The fusion of fingers and ivory, the silk of your touch,
 the flux of your notes outpoured –
Crash of chords, soaring of scales, swirl of arpeggios.
I rehearse birdlike trills at the top and exploit the throaty
 resonance of your bass strings;
Play and foreplay, they are all the same: you stir beneath my
 philandering fingers.
So much latent passion is there to unleash, so inveigling
 is the invitation to surrender!

My contriving is clumsy.
But you are hard-wired to reveal the genius of the composers:
You enable the rages of Beethoven, the repartee of Mozart,
     the heavenly singing of Schubert,
     the sad rubatos of Chopin, the susurrations of Debussy,
     the contrapuntal soul-searchings of J. S. Bach...

You indulgently permit my extemporizing, my probing for
     harmonies, my flirting with dissonances;
You hold to my moods, accepting the sobs and the
     hosannas alike;
You conspire with me in composition,
     colluding with my vain searching for the lost chord;
You chide me for my glibness, you console me in my failures,
     you baulk at my wrong notes -
A friend, you are, for all seasons.
Your sound creeps into the crevices of the soul.

November 2014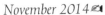

Right: D. A. E. H. - Portrait by Jill Tracey - Rhodesia 1962
Below: The 1899 Steinway calls!

THE SCREAM

(By Edvard Munch, 1893)

'The Scream' describes a moment of personal existential crisis. Munch
described the occasion: "I was walking down the road with two friends,
when the sun set. Suddenly the sky turned red as blood, I stopped and
leant against the fence, feeling desperately tired. Tongues of fire
and blood stretched over the bluish, black fjord. I shivered with fear.
Then I heard the enormous, infinite scream of nature." July 2012 ✍

It troubles me, that silent scream
   Whose horror fills the sky –
The garish light, the lurid gleam,
The foul miasma of a dream,
   The unheard, piteous cry.

Blood flows, tongues of fire glimmer,
   Beyond the blue-black creek
Coloured dissonances shimmer,
   Drowned in that dreadful shriek.

Heard howls are hard upon the ears
   But unheard ones are harder.
See - on that puddle of pale tears
The spectre ship a rumour bears
   Of some unseen armada.

And those two figures, what are they -
   Some direful fate portending?
Darkly they move towards their prey,
   Their closeness seeming to convey
A cataclysmic ending.

The ghoulish, pale, light-bulb head
      An unknown terror grips:
The stare, demented in its dread,
Eyeballs from which the sense has fled,
Ears shut, mouth mouthing things unsaid,
      An oval of black lips.

Who is this soul in agony
      From human likeness changed?
Age? colour? sex? no sign I see
Betraying its anonymity;
Androgynous! how can it be
      So awesomely deranged?

I think I know that soundless cry,
      That deafening emission:
Its echoes pulse upon the eye,
Those swirling contours in the sky:
The soul, seeing all flesh must die,
      Has glimpsed its own perdition.

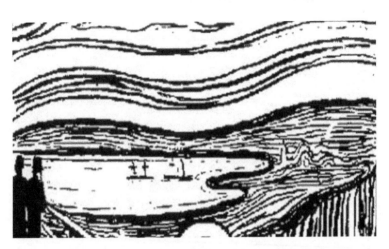

RETURN

"Return" has such a comfortable sound,
The warm iambic speaks of coming home
And breathes contentment, hedges us around
With recognitions, - something of our own.

As music's cadence has the final say
And tonic chord resolves all questings past,
The searching melody has found the way
Back to its home, and closure at the last.

The erring son - the prodigal - returned
To the forgiveness of a father's hearth,
To reconciliation hardly earned,
Love unconditional - and fatted calf.

Adam and Eve could not but vainly rue
Their disobedience, at prodigious cost:
"The world was all before them" – yet they knew
No going back, their Paradise was lost

Lot's wife, fatally tempted as she fled
To look behind her, seeing her city burn,
Was rooted where she stood, no way ahead -
Never to go nor ever to return.

"Return!" The word has a reposeful feeling,
Four walls around, a sheltering roof above -
And, many of our deepest needs revealing,
Recalls the domesticities we love,
Sights that restore and sounds of gentle healing,
Purr of the cat and cooing of a dove.

October 2015

HARK! HARK!

I was about ten when I wrote this poem. I am no ornithologist but I still remember the joy of that birdsong.

Hark! Hark! A chaffinch or a lark?
I hear a song so shrill and long,
So gay and debonair.
A robin or a thrush?
I only know this much –
That someone's feeling mighty good up there!

1945 ✍

FRINGILLA.—(Lat. *a Finch.*)

Cœlebs (Lat. *Bachelor*), *the Chaffinch.*

I was fourteen when I wrote this poem, published in Ramsey Courier and Northern Advertiser. - April 1949

FRIDAY, MAY 6th, 1949.

YOUNG VISITOR'S IMPRESSIONS

David Hunt, aged 14, a schoolboy, of Marlborough College, Wiltshire, who spent his Easter holidays in Ramsey with his parents, wrote the following verses in appreciation of the Island during his stay:

"Whether in England or Ireland,
Or pacing the rocky Welsh banks,
Or over the bonny Scotch borders—
My heart's in the land of the Manx.

I come not from England or Wales,
I am not of fierce Scottish clan,
My homeland is not rugged Ireland,
I come from the Isle of Man."

2

PLACES

❖

TIBET, TIBET

Following the Chinese invasion of 1959, Tibet was taken over, its Buddhist traditions being systematically destroyed. On our visit in 2004 we witnessed part of the final brutal takeover. My apologies to J. Milton Hayes, who wrote 'The Green Eye of the Yellow God', *which begins:*
   'There's a one-eyed yellow idol to the north of Kathmandu…'

There's a land of many idols to the north of Kathmandu,
   A land the world finds easy to forget;
There are monasteries and stupas,* and religion brave and true
   In the wounded, shackled country called Tibet.

Beyond the mountain ranges, where the air is cold and thin,
   Where the sky and stony desert ever meet,
Where the coloured prayer-flags flutter, in a landscape bare
   and grim,
There's a centuries-old tradition in retreat.

Where once the Dalai Lama was revered through all the land,
   Where in former times His Holiness was king,
There has come a jealous wrath, from out the distant north –
   A chill wind is blowing from Beijing.

And monasteries are mouldering across the ruined land,
   In Lhasa Tibetan blood has run;
There are thousands who have died, in a monstrous genocide –
   The deed of desecration has been done.

There are foreigners in multitudes along the city streets,
   There are red flags in the villages – and yet
The people (humbler, poorer) still devoutly do the Kora*
   Round the ancient, holy places of Tibet.

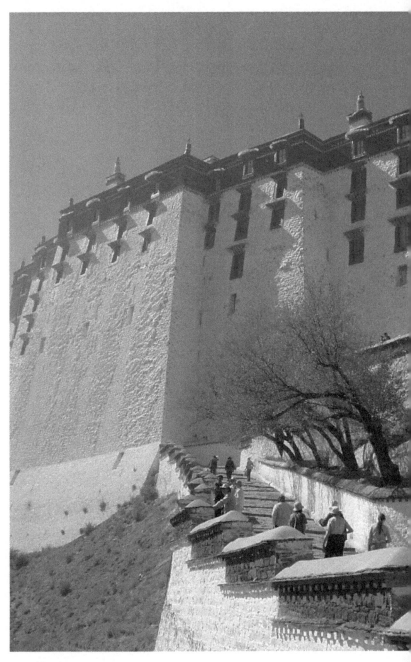

The Potala, Lhasa

The limitless horizons have become their prison walls,
    Over Chomolungma's* snows the sun has set.
But 'OM MANI PADME HUM'*, the ancient mantra, ever calls
    To those who care to hear, beyond Tibet.

Your faces, lined and wrinkled – "Tashi Delay!"* – creased in smiles,
    Your yaks, your shrines, your palaces, your tents,
Your venerated lamas, your predestinated karmas,*
    Your great Potala – pinnacled, immense -

Your singing-bowls, your dorjes,* beads and aprons, khatag scarves,*
    Your lofty Buddha's smile serenely set,
Your gentleness, devotion, and your prayer-wheels in motion –
    All these, perhaps, will one day save Tibet.

That land of many idols to the north of Kathmandu
    Is a place the world finds easy to forget.
But WE have seen a people undefeated, brave and true:
    We will remember you – Tibet! Tibet!

June 2004☙

STUPA: a Buddhist shrine, KORA: a pilgrims' procession round a holy place, always clockwise, CHOMOLUNGMA: the Tibetan name for Everest, 'OM MANI PADME HUM": sacred mantra, TASHI DELAY: Tibetan greeting, KARMA: the fate that decides your next incarnation, DORJE; representation of a thunderbolt, KHATAG: silk scarf presented as token of respect, THE POTALA: the erstwhile palace of the Dalai Lama in Lhasa.

HAMPI

*Composed after a visit to Hampi and the ruins of Vijayanagar
('City of Victory'), the capital of a great Hindu empire which flourished
in the 14th, 15th and 16th centuries and dominated much of South
India, commercially and militarily, and whose one active temple is still
a pilgrimage centre today. It is set in the midst of a vast, boulder-strewn
wilderness in the centre of Karnataka, a 350-mile drive from Goa,
where we were staying. A musician tapped tunes on musical pillars.
Priests buffeted a barren woman and a performing elephant blessed
us with his trunk.*

A dazzling city once - Vijayanagar,
        Where traders, warriors, pilgrims came in droves:
Today a ruined dream, forgotten saga,
        Empty, midst boulders and banana groves.

Here, where a city's ancient pride still smoulders
        - Pavilions, temples, treasures from the past –
We watched, among those monumental boulders,
        The sun set blood-red on an empire vast.

What visionary? What transcendent dreamer?
        What sculptor, faith-possessed, was moved to make
This monolithic, scowling Narasimha*
        Seated for ever on his coiled snake?

Among the courtly palaces and villas
        The great Vitthala Temple ruins stand –
Stone chariot, music-making pillars,
        Voluptuous carvings, faith-inspired and grand.➥

And here, alive in all its present power,
    The Virupaksha - pilgrims still abound:
Above, its soaring mighty Gopuram tower;
    Below, its priests, prostrations on the ground

And holy men, and rituals with the ability
    To help a woman desperate to conceive;
An elephant whose very versatility
    Persuades the unbeliever to believe!

These, the sole relics of a mighty city
    Where men of power and wealth and men of prayer
Shared once a life – its glory and its pity,
    And left an Indian dowry rich and rare.

Narasimha: avatar of Vishnu
February 2006

Virupaksha Temple, Hampi, Karnataka

ASSISI

To the green heart of Italy, to Umbria we came,
Where poets, painters, popes and saints found resonating fame –
A land of fortresses, cathedrals, terraced vineyards, farms,
And battlefields where once there sounded many a call to arms.
Among these groves a city lives – apart, but not aloof,
Assisi, fundamental halt upon the path to truth.

You painters of Perugia, you knew this Umbrian light,
You caught the chasing shadows and the colours, brittle, bright.
Today Giotto's frescoes are more eloquent than words
To show the gentle power of Francis preaching to the birds.
'Mid homely Umbrian landscapes sacred pageants burst upon us –
Nativities, Annunciations, Martyrs, meek Madonnas –
And medieval piety with joyous passion fills
The wide skies and the wooded slopes of Umbria's rolling hills.

Assisi, heart of Christendom, climbs from Spoleto's vale
To Mount Subasio – and heights that Francis dared to scale.
Your son was here, taught men to love the poorest of the poor,
Himself a singing *poverello*, God's own troubadour.
Your ancient stones of pink and grey such saintliness enhances
As calls all pilgrims from all lands to emulate St Francis –
The one who canticled the Sun, who was of fire baptised,
A man whose hands and feet were shown bloodily stigmatised,
A monk attired in nakedness, example to us all...

...But men have looked the other way and Umbrian shadows fall
Upon the sainted figure those Renaissance painters made,
So passionately loved, revered, so tenderly portrayed.
And Perugino's brush is dry, gone is Giotto's muse –

Yet Francis still lives on amid those joyous frescoed hues,
And Brother Sun and Sister Moon and all our fellow creatures
Bear witness to the inconvenient truth this monk can teach us.

O Francis, show us here, among the spired cypress trees,
The silvery olive groves, the vines, the passing things that please,
How poverty-stricken-rich we are - and drive us to our knees!

June 2009

St Francis of Assisi

MULL

Composed after the Salen Show.

A gentle Hebridean twilight steals across the Sound,
   Silenced is every heron, curlew, gull;
The hills of Scotland, sunset-touched, stand sentinel around
   The steep, unpeopled solitudes of Mull.

The Show is over now, the stock and judges have dispersed –
   The thoroughbreds so delicately reared,
The Highland cattle's shaggy splendour, diligently nursed,
   The jostling tups and ewes so plumply sheared.

Grey, creeper-clad, upon a bluff the ruined castle stands
   Among the oyster-catchers, rocks and reeds,
Witness to eight hundred years of battles, chiefs and clans –
   Lords of the Isles, their fell and bloody deeds.

Island of ritual monuments, of chambered cairns and mounds,
   Of standing stones and Neolithic graves,
Of glaciated glens and sedimentary rocky Sounds,
   Columns of basalt swept bare by the waves.

A Spanish galleon, decked in the Armada's pride and glory,
   Sank here - a treasure tale still told and sung -
Where rainbow-coloured houses throng the quays of Tobermory
   And Islanders still talk the Gaelic tongue.

Far to the west a summons clear – Iona's holy isle!
   The churning waters pave the ancient way
To St Colomba's refuge, where the Abbey's granite pile
   Calls pilgrim souls to contemplate and pray.

The bulk of Ben More broods in clouds above the sunlit lochs,
   Beached on its headland crouches Duart's hull;
A land of seals and deer and eagles, moors and fens and rocks,
A place whose ancient mysteries no incomer unlocks -
   This craggy, talismanic isle of Mull.

August 2012

Above: Duart Castle, Mull

SHARROW

Following a visit to Haywards Heath in April 2014, when I was shocked to find my old home due for demolition.

This was my home - this grey, abandoned place –
This was my start, the 'rock whence I was hewn'.
Of those far days there soon will be no trace,
Save memories, amongst the rubble strewn.

For it was here, with aspirations fine,
That my devoted parents – long since dead –
Occupied Sharrow, putting up a sign:
"School for the Sons of Gentlemen", it said.

The 'Big Lawn', where the Wellingtonia tree,
Towered tremendously above the fray;
The 'Small Lawn'. where we children could be free
To dig the sandpit, swing aloft, and play;
The rhododendrons, each bush the trustee
Of secrets, where our fancies held full sway.

The chicken-run, the quaint-shaped swimming pool,
The orchard's apple trees we loved to climb;
The house, that was at once both home and school;
The uncharted corners – wilderness sublime! –
All subject now to demolition's rule,
Soft targets for the onward march of time.➤

Sharrow as last seen. (Inset: In happier days with Stripes our donkey)

The 'night-nursery', where – after prayers – I slept;
The backstairs, drab with dark linoleum browns;
The scullery, where scoured pans were kept,
The drawing-room, with views of Sussex Downs.
The nursery wing, where Nanny reigned supreme,
A guarantee against high standards slipping -
While downstairs Cook's benevolent régime
Supplied illicit scraps of bread-and-dripping.

And it was here we watched the War go by
And heard the dreaded 'Doodlebugs' at night,
Saw parachutists falling from the sky
While sirens sent us scurrying in fright
To cellars dark, while battles raged on high,
Until the 'All Clear' called us back to light.

All is now gone - or else about to go:
The place is ringed with car-parks for the shops
And demolition signs make joyless show.
Development, I see, at nothing stops.

And so this place, possessor of my past,
By asset-stripping progress overtaken,
Is soon to vanish, freed from ghosts at last,
My childhood haunts forgotten and forsaken.
The bulldozers are here, the die is cast:
The ground, which I thought firm, is sorely shaken.

April 2014 ✎

Sharrow School in its heyday - 1939

EATON HALL

National Service at Officer Cadet Training School, Chester.

The part I most remember of my time at Eaton Hall
    (Where the Duke of Westminster owned every inch)
Is the sound, on the parade ground - all too easy to recall –
    Of Regimental Sergeant-Major Lynch.

He liked to have us marking time – so fast it was absurd! –
    His barbs of wit still chillingly resound;
When I was out of step (which all too frequently occurred):
    "Who's that little man with both feet off the ground?"

He informed us that the C.O. is always in the right,
    No matter how outrageously he lies:
"If he says the sun is shining in the middle of the night,
    Then what yer do, yer bloody shields yer eyes!"

The importance of the RSM was clear at Eaton Hall –
    Though hard to understand unless you'd seen it:
"I call YOU 'sir', you call ME 'sir'", is what he told us all,
    "The only difference being that YOU mean it."

For infantry cadets it was as warlike as it gets,
    With bayonet drill essential for attacks:
We played out all our dreams and with raw, blood-curdling
                            screams
    We plunged our bayonets into well-stuffed sacks

For battle tactics to the North Welsh mountains we would go;
 There came about the accident we feared,
When someone lost his rifle in a waist-high drift of snow
 And the hapless, careless culprit was cashiered.

The guardroom was a gaol for mistakes beyond the pale;
 For lesser crimes there was a running track:
Did the sprinting do us good? Well, we managed as we could
 Those two miles to the Obelisk and back.

Titled 'Officers and Gentlemen', we wore our pips with pride,
 In style we passed out, those who did not fall:
We learned a deal of discipline and much more on the side
 'Mid the splendid marbled vaults of Eaton Hall.

I'd not go back there now (being considerably older),
 Whatever prize the Army might bestow.
They say there's nothing bolder than a pip upon one's shoulder
 But an officer has something more to show:
We learnt how not to flinch,
 under Sergeant-Major Lynch -
 I've BEEN there,
 DONE that,
 sixty years ago!

April 2014

Parade at Eaton Hall

CAMBRIDGE

A sonnet.

When I recall those careless Cambridge days
And wistfully re-trace my youthful tracks,
All is compounded in a golden haze
Of sunlit lawns and blossom on the Backs

And dons and gowns – badges of education,
Lectures and books, parties and prankish flings,
Tutorials, girls and nervous expectation,
May Balls, the Bumps - and Evensong at King's

And bicycles (the mode that never varies)
And ghosts of Cambridge men whose deeds still shine
And churches, from St Giles' to Great St Mary's,
And Milton's rooms directly next to mine!

And yet – God help me! – a much longer list
Shows all the opportunities I missed.

September 2013

Above: King's College, Cambridge and Senate House on Graduation Day.

KALAMAKI - CORFU

Our daughter's family villa, scene of many holidays.

There's a full moon riding high above the calm Ionian Sea,
Where a Kalamaki villa is so dear to you and me,
With the promise of tomorrow's leisure, pleasure-filled and free –
    And Corfu once again has cast its spell.
There are wavelets lapping lazily along the empty beach
And the mountains of Albania are ranged beyond our reach:
Two seashores face each other, twinkling gently each to each.
    There's harmony by moonlight. All is well.

Impregnable, this island fortress spurned barbarian raiders
And stoutly it repelled assaults by Ottoman invaders –
Five centuries of bargains struck with traders and crusaders,
    It boasts a fearsome heritage – and fine.
Four hundred years these islands to Venetian rule were bound,
Then came the French, whose architectural vistas still are found –
Till Britain dashed Napoleon's hopes, installed a cricket ground,
    Where Corfiots sit and sip their kumquat wine.

Night comes – but for his worshippers the sun is lying in wait;
Tomorrow the expensive yachts will ply along the strait
And to our jetty ferries will offload their human freight –
    Corfu will work its miracle once more.
And Corfu colours, smells and tastes to all the senses pander:
Its oranges and lemons, olive groves and jacaranda,
Geraniums, bougainvillea, orchids, oleander –
    Its riches flow unchecked from every pore.

Here, legend has it, Ulysses sailed from the Trojan War,
Was shipwrecked, was washed up upon this island's rocky shore:
Poseidon turned his ship to stone, such was the grudge he bore,
    And here for Ithaca Odysseus pined.
And here, as Shakespeare has it, lived old Prospero in his cave:
"O brave new world!" Miranda cried, such joy the island gave!
Corfu today is still a world forever new and brave –
    Like Spyridon, its silver saint enshrined.
    What lovelier place could anybody find?

June 2016 🏴

Above: The infinity pool, Kalamaki
Right: a sketch of a villa courtyard
entrance 2016

ON RETURNING TO CORNWALL

Bude was the scene of many childhood holidays.

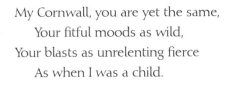

My Cornwall, you are yet the same,
    Your fitful moods as wild,
Your blasts as unrelenting fierce
    As when I was a child.

Still stings the spray on Cornish cliff
    And still the seagulls scream
Their harsh, unceasing threnody
    Upon a dismal theme.

Still may I climb the gritty rocks
    To echoing, thund'rous caves
And watch along the flat, wet sands
    The serried ranks of waves.

Who walks the darken'd beach still hears
    The orchestrated might
Of seas whose gusty music fills
    The vaulted halls of night.

Still, Cornwall, has your sobbing voice
    The power to give me joy -
Tumultuous your breaking waves
    As when I was a boy.

1975

ON A CORNISH BEACH

(inspired by Linda's painting)

*An artistic friend presented me with her remarkably evocative painting of
a seascape on a stormy day, with huge waves and a lowering sky and a
single indistinct figure on the sands. She tells me it is in Northumberland
– but to me it is the Cornwall of my youth!*

The picture makes a deafening noise, its clamour draws me in:
The artist's brush assaults my ears with that tremendous din.
I hear the all-embracing sounds – the sea's primordial roar,
The crash of breakers, surge of surf on that forsaken shore.

I hear the thunder in the wind, the gulls' demented scream,
The unremitting backlash of the waves venting their spleen.
All this I hear – and on my cheek I feel the stinging spray
And view the crested sea, white horses galloping away.

Breathless I gasp, my heaving lungs are filled with salty air,
The wind's shrill blast is in my ears, the sand is in my hair,
I breast that troubled firmament, surreal in its gloom,
I count the serried ranks of waves, I taste the flying spume.

And then, upon the untamed scene, a human shape appears,
A child's form seen mistily through tempest-driven tears ! –
Or are my tears quite otherwise, tears for a world that's passed?
I am that child, revisiting those carefree years at last!

For this to me is Cornwall – and these are Cornish sands,
This the horizon where in vain I searched for foreign lands
Thinking that just across the bay Africa could be found -
And this the beach where we would play, not yet by
                                         caution bound
Though often told that rip-tides ruled and children could
                                         be drowned.

Beyond this intumescent sea, beyond the ebb and flow,
Beyond the dark horizon and its eldritch, lingering glow
Imagination soars, I take the ages in my stride:
Once more I am in Cornwall, building castles 'gainst the tide
And scanning every battling wave for one which I might ride:
A salt-drenched, elemental joy! The child that never died!

October 2017 ✍

3
UPLANDS

❖

CUMBRIA

(With apologies to Kipling and to Sussex)

God gave all men all earth to love,
    But since our hearts are small,
Ordained for each one spot should prove
    Beloved over all.
Each to his choice, but I rejoice,
    With every dawn that breaks,
In a fair ground, in a fair ground,
    Yea, Cumbria and the Lakes.

On Sussex Downs the sun shines warm,
    Where blows the genial breeze.
But when a sudden southern storm
    Ruffles the dappled seas,
Then – when I hear the thunder roll
    And the wind howl in the hearth –
My thoughts fly northwards, and my soul
    Cries for a stony path.

Here, where dark crags overawe
    And swirling mists perplex,
Our herdwicks graze, and kestrels soar
    Above the tumbling becks.
No level pebbled beach is here,
    No chalky downland swells,
No gentle sunlit slopes to cheer –
    Only the brooding fells.

Our boundaries are the drystone walls,
    No accommodating hedge,
No charitable breeze – but squalls
    Gust over Striding Edge.
And Wastwater is deep and black,
    And bare of bush or tree,
Along its banks a crooked track
    Across a bouldered scree.

I will walk up against the winds
    Till bones and muscles ache,
Where the Old Man of Coniston
    Looms high above the Lake.
I shall see waters glint like glass,
See where proud Scafell stands,
See how the way from Wrynose Pass
Drops down to Duddon Sands.

Give me the bawling waterfalls
That drive the lonely mills,
The flinty farms, the crumbling walls
    And Wordsworth's daffodils.
Each to his choice! but I rejoice
With every dawn that breaks,
In a fair ground, in a fair ground,
Yea, Cumbria and the Lakes.

May 2007

FELL FEVER

With apologies to John Masefield and his fine poem 'Sea Fever'

I must up to the fells again, to the lonely fells and the sky,
And all I ask is a stony path and a gabbling beck nearby
And a dry-stone wall and a stile to climb and the crunch of
                          the brown-dead bracken
And a keening cry from the high scar where the shadows blacken.

I must up to the fells again, for the call of the misty heights
Is a clear call and a wild call, as wild as the wheeling kites;
And all I ask is a lichened rock, and a bouldered summit thrusting
And a grey mist on a mountain top and a chill wind gusting.

I must up to the fells again, to the Cumbrian walker's ways,
To the lonely fells and the dark fells where pale-faced
                          Herdwicks graze;
And all I ask is a panting pause for a glimpse of the vision splendid –
And aching limbs and a hot bath when the long hike's ended.

August 2010

FELL WALKING

We belong to a weekly walking group, the Pilgrims.

To walking the Pilgrims are strangely attracted;
Good leadership? Yes, and they never have lacked it.
A challenging peak? They have often attacked it.
A Hard Knott to crack? And behold! they have cracked it!
What lovelier spot could a man wish to dwell in?
Of so many foot-slogging walks there's no telling –
The rocks that we slipped on, the bogs that we fell in -
Not to mention Blencathra, Skiddaw and Helvellyn!

What price does one pay for the height one attains
And the view, from the top, of the valleys and plains?
Just a blister or two and a chill through and through
When it blows and it blasts and it snows and it rains,
While elderly joints take the stresses and strains
And the cramps come along, and the aches and the pains,
And only the obstinate will-power remains
And the losses seem very much more than the gains.

Yet we say, with a smile, that it's all worth the while,
The rain-clouds perverse will in good time disperse,
The storm will blow over, the drizzle will fizzle,
At the end of the day they will all go away –
For the call of the Cumbrian fells never fails:
We claim as our kingdom the hills and the vales!

January 2012

HIGH ON OUR FELLS

High on our fells the air is bracing and thin
      And great winds blow
And keen-cutting cold is harsh on the skin
      And faces glow.

And lonely it is on the fells where, unblinkingly eyeing us,
      The Herdwicks say:
"What brings this raggedy, muffled procession of climbers
      On their halting way?"

Once crofters and poets and Roman legions
      Walked these heights.
Today we, too, on the same proud regions
      Have set our sights.

And today on the fells, in the wet and the wind and the wailing,
      This is our prayer:
These beckoning crests may we long be scaling
      And the mountains bare.

November 2009

70

BLENCATHRA

A confessional poem.

It was an act of hubris, my ascent.
Blencathra's towering grandeur drew me on:
To make it to the summit I was bent –
The sun, on my ambition, falsely shone.
Those shattered cliffs both beckon and repel,
That ancient bouldered fortress summons all –
But since I've been up many a Cumbrian fell,
I failed to see Pride comes before a Fall.

Alas! I made it to the top all right
(The panorama was the goal I sought) -
But coming down from that commanding height
My legs, quite simply, withdrew their support.
Half carried home, I was a sorry sight:
I find my flesh is frailer than I thought.

August 2014

LAKE DISTRICT WET

There is a universal perception of the Lake District as a place where it mostly rains. So be it!

I would not have it any other way.
This place I love, here's where I hope to stay –
High on this hill, where everything impels
The wandering eye to fasten on the fells,
The sweet contours of Coniston Old Man.
Its paths I trace, its cliffs and quarries scan
And glimpse, over its shoulder, Scafall Pike
And recollect some long, now distant, hike.
And though our skies be often leaden-grey
And though pervading wetness wins the day,
I would not have it any other way.

To climb Helvellyn was a youthful pledge:
We made the ascent by way of Striding Edge –
A scramble in the tempest's very teeth,
Storm overhead and swirling mists beneath,
Dizzy the drop, fearsome the noisy fray
Of helicopter rescue kept at bay,
While, far below, Red Tarn in waiting lay.
Stalked by the rain, soaked in the cascade's spray,
I would not have it any other way.

I once, alone, climbed Skiddaw in bright weather,
Its slopes were purpled all with springing heather,
Its noble bulk bestriding Keswick vale,
Blencathra, Bassenthwaite and Borrowdale.

Then sudden dark encroached upon the day
And Derwentwater's sparkling face turned grey
And Cat Bells caught the sun's last brilliant ray
And rain squalls came and took the sight away.
Such brave, storm-threaten'd splendour does not stay,
Nor would I have it any other way.

Then there's Wastwater, deepest of them all,
Profoundly still, its depths too deep to trawl,
Quiescent at the foot of Scafell's screes,
Its surface black, its banks bereft of trees.
It mirrors forth Great Gable's mighty sway,
Its silence reprimands the unclouded day,
It broods – and brings forth rain. And so they say
Inclemency must be the price we pay
And - though the heavens may open every day -
We may not have it any other way.
I would not have it any other way!

September 2016

ON GUMMERS HOW

A personal view.

Gummers How is a small fell near us from which a panoramic view is to be had, across Windermere, of most of the Cumbrian peaks. (I have indeed seen all the places mentioned!)

Full many a glorious mountain-top I've seen
Where sky and earth in mighty congress meet.
On Kilimanjaro's cratered peak I've been –
All Africa lay boundless at my feet.

On Kanchenjunga's sacred slopes I've trekked,
Breathless upon a Himalayan height,
And seen the world's roof, all in snow bedecked -
Makalu, Lhotse, Nuptse – awesome sight!

I've seen on walls of ice the silhouette
Of Annapurna's battlemented crest.
From Rhombu Glacier in high Tibet
I've seen the spindrift flow off Everest.

At rosy dawn I've seen Mount Fuji float,
Detached most delicately from the land below.
The Rockies, too, primordial and remote –
Across the plains I've seen their shadows go.

I've seen the Matterhorn the heavens flout,
With pyramidal splendour girt about.
I've seen, beyond Sahara hot and dry,
The snowy Atlas holding up the sky;
Seen Table Mountain, draped in cloth of grey,
Massively crouched above a city's fray.

And yet no sight is nobler or more dear
Than, seen from Gummers How when skies are clear,
The fells of Cumbria over Windermere.

January 2016.

SANDAKPHU

(with apologies to T.S.Eliot and G.K.Chesterton).

We trekked to Sandakphu, a ridge at 13,000ft in the shadow of Kanchenjunga, from which is gained a panoramic view of the Everest range.

A hard coming we had of it,
  A steep, relentless way;
An upward struggle we had of it
  Day after slogging day.
A labour of love we made of it,
  This thing we had to do –
The day we sought for Everest
  By way of Sandakphu.

And passing friends we made of them,
  The villagers we met –
Hill people, Gurkhas, Nepalese
  And folk from high Tibet.
Their smiling stopped us in our tracks
  And warmed our chilled bones through,
While softly chimed the bells of yaks
  On the way to Sandakphu.

Close was the forest's canopy,
  The way grew darker, eerier,
Broad-leafed magnolia, chestnut oaks,
  Deodars, cryptomeria…
Our path with lichen'd rocks was strewn;
  Trunks from which orchids flower'd
Stood all around and – dark at noon –
  The rhododendrons tower'd.

And then the sunny uplands came,
   We drank the thin air, deep.
The swift streams trilled, cicadas shrilled,
   Our panting path was steep…
Until the night – ah, welcome sight,
   A village! – and, hard by,
A solitary yak, outlined
   Against a sunset sky.

Joyous, we sang a song of it
   Where plunging vales resound;
Humbled, we made a prayer of it –
   For this was holy ground:
The dark ravines, the soaring heights,
   The very stones we trod,
The distant eagles' wheeling flights
   Brushing the face of God ☛

We looked for Him and found Him there
  Amid the glist'ning crags,
With white-washed chortens, lonely shrines
  And fluttering prayer-flags.
And monkish chanting filled the air
  'Neath Kanchenjunga's snows –
The mountain multi-faceted,
  The home the spirits chose.

With ev'ning mists about her flanks,
  Impenetrable shrouds,
The mighty Kanchenjunga's face
  Showed high above the clouds.
So long the climb, so short the breath,
  So limitless the view!
The day we sought for Everest
  By way of Sandakphu.

And Sandakphu gave us her boon –
  A sunrise scene unfurl'd:
Peak after silent peak caught fire
  On the very roof of the world!
We stood in awe, spectators small –
  Such pageantry sublime! –
In that lonely, cold, exalted place
  At the world's great morning-time.

❖ ❖ ❖ ❖ ❖ 🖝

A hard descent we had of it,
  Returning from the crest;
Down, down we steeply came from it
  Where painful knees protest.
A labour of love we made of it,
  This thing we had to do,
The day we came to Everest
  By way of Sandakphu.

November 1997

Above: Everest and a Tibetan yak print block.

THE CLIMB

With thanks to Robert Browning and to George Mallory, of Everest fame -

The mountain top is all I ask,
    No one could want for more.
"A man's reach should exceed his grasp –
    Or what's a Heaven for?"

O mountaineer, why must you climb
    That peak which few men dare?
The answer, simple but sublime:
    "Because it's there!"

January 2015

Annapurna's Fishtail Mountain, Nepal

4
FANDANGLES

❖

AN APPLE IS A TOOTHSOME THING

An apple is a toothsome thing, God wot! -
As curious Eve discovered, to her cost,
And Adam, too, did fall for Satan's plot:
They knew full well the boundary they had crossed.

The kindness of his Maker Man forgot:
Small wonder, then, that Paradise was Lost!

November 2016

THE GLASS

Some folk lead lives of cheerful equanimity
While some a long face are inclined to pull:
These are the ones who see the glass half empty;
Thank God for those who fancy it half full!

November 2016

BANKERS MAKE FORTUNES

Bankers make fortunes,
Bees make honey,
Farmers make hay
While the weather is sunny,
Divers make waves
And (which is funny)
Potters make pots –
But not of money!

December 2016

TOOTHACHE

Hell hath no fury like a nagging tooth:
      It gnaws the very vitals, like a curse.
No greater ire hath Hellfire – but forsooth!
      The rage of raging toothache's even worse!
Extraction cures it all, to tell the truth,
      And I can now make light of it in verse.

July 2017

THE CHRISTMAS CARD ROBIN

The robin on a Christmas card is a bit of a cliché but at least it's cheerful.

Here's an archetypal robin on an archetypal twig
    Lending colour to the archetypal snow.
'Mid snowflakes fiercely dancing in a complicated jig
    A robin redbreast makes a gallant show.
This ruffled little bird will need a larder in his gizzard
    For a meal when the settled snow is hard,
But for now he's just a lovesome smudge of scarlet in the blizzard
    For an archetypal 'Happy Christmas' card!

December 2016

"CONSUBSTANTIAL, CO-ETERNAL"

"Consubstantial, co-eternal,
     While unending ages run."
Although of truth the very kernel,
     Such words baffle everyone.

"Consubstantial, co-eternal" -
     Yet, although the words sound great,
Explaining would fill up a journal -
     Is there someone can translate?

"Consubstantial, co-eternal" –
     To clarify it language fails:
Is the afterlife infernal –
     Gnashing teeth and endless wails?
Or is it bliss, with choirs supernal
     Chorusing like nightingales?

"Consubstantial, co-eternal"
     No one really comprehends!
Life internal, death external?
Light nocturnal? dark diurnal?
Consubstantial? Co-eternal? -
     One thing's sure: it never ends!

November 2016✍

MY HEART LEAPS UP

(With apologies to Wordsworth's rainbow)

My heart leaps up when I behold
    A porker in the sky.
So be it! I am likewise told
I'll not be geriatric old
Nor lose the plot, nor feel the cold
Nor find my bladder's uncontrolled.
Yes, old age is a pot of gold –
    So long as pigs can fly.

October 2016

HELLFIRE

The preacher preached hellfire and brimstone and horror,
    He ranted, he warmed to his theme:
Of Sodom he spoke, and the fate of Gomorrah –
    Of hope there was never a gleam.

"There'll be wailing and gnashing of teeth"and he glared,
    "Your fate is already decided!"
Just then one old lady cried, suitably scared,
"I ain't got no teeth". But the preacher declared:
    "No problem! False teeth are provided!"

July 2017

NEVER

A poem composed in twenty minutes at a poetry session (I was given the title 'Never') at the Wordsworth Trust, Grasmere, November 2010

George Washington declared "I never lied".
The thing's impossible! "I never died"
Could truthfully be said (though, better, "I've not died -
Yet").
Consider it a moment from my side:
How COULD a man, however hard he tried,
Say honestly that he had never lied?

"The Pope is never wrong", the Catholics say,
"The Pope's whole point is his infallibility" –
But that's sheer folly! Look at it this way:
The Pope's a wise man, claiming the facility
To know God's purpose – yet he COULD be wrong!
"Never"'s a word too definite, too strong.

Buying on the never-never is ill planned
When it is clear your assets are all shrinking.
Some say that Hell's a Never-Never Land:
That COULD be true – or could be wishful thinking.
"Never say die" was what the Captain said
As his ship was going down - then sank like lead.

But wait! There IS a viable occasion
When someone not dogmatic or too clever,
Without pretence or lying or evasion,
Being taken by surprise, says "Well I never!"

SLOUGH

With apologies to John Betjeman, whose poem begins "Come. friendly bombs, and fall on Slough" – which did not make him popular in that town!

There was a young person of Slough
Who denounced "friendly bombs" and "the plough":
    Said he "Have no fear,
    Our town is still here –
And where are YOU, Betjeman, now?!"

LOT'S WIFE

There was a young migrant whose fault
Brought her flight to a permanent halt.
    But the tale of her turning
    To see Sodom burning
We may take with a large pinch of…
    …the proverbial condiment!

SKEGNESS

There was a young man of Skegness
Who spent his life trying to impress:
    Folk flocked to his door,
    He was praised more and more –
But alas! he was liked less and less!

I once entered a limerick competition set by Famous Grouse Whisky, in which the winner would receive a case of whisky. Unfortunately my contribution arrived after the deadline. I like to think I might have done well!

FAMOUS GROUSE

A bigamist drank Famous Grouse
And was flanked on each side by a spouse:
    Asked which he preferred,
    He replied that a bird
In the bottle's worth two in the house.

5

PEOPLE

❖

WILLIAM AND KATE

A prince's heart has to his mistress gone –
A royal match already come to pass.
Not 'Princess' yet, but plain 'Miss Middleton',
Of Middle England, she, and middle class.
No royal blood, no born aristocrat,
No glittering scion of a ducal tree:
A commoner – and none the worse for that!
We love her for her lesser pedigree.
His heart was captured, seven years went by,
Nor would Prince William love at lower rate:
Diana's ring! For love, no price too high;
The whole world loves to love her – "Kiss me, Kate!"

So 'twould be strange if, 'mid the jubilation,
The married state should die across the nation!

November 2010

94

JUSTIN IN SWITZERLAND

aged 9 months

So young you were, amid the eternal snows,
    Your laughter kindled by a distant sound –
Sweet dissonance of far-off cattle-bells:
    The ageless mountains ring'd you all around.

You laughed again – this time some secret cause,
    Some sudden, passing figment of your mind
Called forth your laughter. Sternly stood the hills
    Silent before your innocence, and blind.

And truth to tell, those mighty sentinels,
    Those buttress'd shining summits undefiled,
Are less a wonder, less a miracle
    Than this – the sudden laughter of a child.

Autumn 1968

"I CAN'T NOT"

My wife's endemic weakness

"I can't NOT" is what she said when I questioned her stated
    intention to answer a neighbour's inconvenient call for help.

"I can't NOT" is ungrammatical, a double negative,
    a contradiction in terms.
On the other hand it is powerful and unambiguous.

"I can't NOT" expresses a compulsion,
    a moral obligation not to be denied.
It indicates a hapless orientation towards doing the right thing,

But would one use it where the temptation is, say, carnal -
    greed, for example?
("I can't NOT grab and consume that éclair."}
Perhaps. But, more likely, "I can't resist it.":
Nothing sacrificial there! Indeed, no desire to resist at all!

Consider the Good Samaritan's inability to pass by on the other side.
"I can't NOT" was his response to the plight of the victim on the ground.
It was total surrender to a divine impulse.
The double negative was indeed a positive. And it led to action.

"I can't NOT" is irrefutable, it brooks no argument,
    will not be gainsaid.
There is no escaping the action or its consequences.
It is foreordained, it is karmic, it is in one's stars.
It is character. It is the way one is made.
It is gut.

"Why expend all your time and energy?" I asked,
"Why all this unrewarded kindness –which runs counter to
    commonsense and only wears you out?"
And she answered "I can't NOT."

You ask me why I am drawing attention to my wife's open heart?
    The answer is: I can't NOT!

October 2016

TRUMP

*(I have discovered that almost every word that rhymes with Trump
has unattractive or unpleasant connotations.)*

It is a universal truth that all may hear and see:
Too many dismal words there are which end with U.M.P.
Too often and repeatedly they give us all the HUMP –
Unpleasant and unpalatable, words that rhyme with TRUMP.

From bliss we must come back to earth – but always with a BUMP.
When angry and frustrated we find somebody to THUMP.
Abject with failure and defeat, into a chair we SLUMP
Or bandy angry words and in high dudgeon off we STUMP.

A dowdy, unattractive woman people call a FRUMP;
A crotchety old man is indisputably a GRUMP;
It's friendly but unflattering to call a fatty "PLUMP";
A clumsy blunder? – that's the hallmark of a silly CHUMP.

Life can be full of setbacks that we simply have to LUMP
(The 'lumpen proletariat' is an unattractive CLUMP).
We shudder when we hear the shells exploding with a CRUMP;
If you should lose an arm or leg you'll boast a bloody STUMP.

And failing banks and falling values signify a SLUMP,
And when you buy a house, beware of those who may GAZUMP.
If there's a place we do not like, we label it a DUMP
Or else we gloss things over – but a cesspool's still a SUMP!

And now we have the man for whom so many voters PLUMP,
Whose witterings and twitterings the world just has to LUMP.
How can we yet contain the urge to kick him up the RUMP? -
The unspeakable, preposterous, outrageous DONALD TRUMP!

PS ❖ ❖ ❖ ❖ ❖ ❖

The Last Trump may not be the last – for there are UMPTEEN TRUMPS:
To make it plural only makes it worse – like catching MUMPS!
And every junior Trump is now presumably a TRUMPET
And TRUMPERY is everywhere – and Fortune is a STRUMPET!

The fact is that the man's still here, the man we'd like to THUMP
Or flush him down a gurgling drain or swamp him in a SUMP,
The man to whom we'd like to say 'Go take a running JUMP!' -
The egregious, the inglorious, the monstrous DONALD TRUMP!

May 2017

99

MY NIGHTINGALE

On the occasion of our 49th Wedding Anniversary.
(Those who trained at St Thomas's Hospital were called Nightingales.)

Where would I be without you,
　　My wife, my dearest limb?
If ever I did doubt you
　　My universe would dim.
You have that truth about you
　　Which tells my soul to sing.

That far day in Darjeeling
　　One meeting changed my life:
My fate that moment sealing:
There came a sudden feeling
　　As sure as surgeon's knife -
　　I knew you for my wife!

Left: Nurse Judith Goddard in uniform.
Below: St Thomas's Hospital - our limited
edition print by David Gentleman of the
view from The Houses of Parliament.

And still we are together,

    Through healthy days – and frail,

A bond which none can sever,

    I have the Holy Grail.

No need for more endeavour!

Caged in my heart for ever

    There sings a Nightingale.

17th December 2015

Holy Trinity Church, Penn - 17th December 1966

The sequel: 50th Anniversary Celebrations in December 2016!

ON THE BIRTH OF OUR DAUGHTER, ANTONIA

(Bulawayo, Rhodesia, 14th May, 1970)

Outside beneath a burnished sky
    The city's bosom swells,
Grows big with child – and "5 o'clock"
    Proclaim the city bells.

This little ward must witness now
    The age-old pangs again –
"In sorrow shalt thou bring forth child
    In travail and in pain."

The fingers clenched, the knuckles white,
    The sharp in-drawing of breath –
"Thy sorrows will I multiply",
    Each birth a taste of death.

The city's fertile womb gives forth
    Its progeny full grown –
And no inducement needed there
    Save pub and club and home!

The shoppers, workers, businessmen
    Are spawned on every street,
The headlights prick the gathering dusk,
    Clerks throng with hurrying feet.

But here is one must labour on,
    No rest where lives are made,
No downing tools at stroke of clock,
    It's overtime – unpaid!

No wages but a surgeon's knife,
    A membrane rudely torn,
An agony – yet puny price
To purchase (what less could suffice?)
This "miracle of rare device" –
    A baby girl newborn.

Now fill this city with more joy
    Than all the church bells can!
And let its twilight peace be riven,
For unto us a child is given –
Praise God who made the earth and heaven
    And "in His image, Man!".

THE EUCALYPTUS

(On my favourite pictures of Judy, pruning the eucalyptus in our garden at Ringmer, East Sussex).

'Twas on a sunlit Sussex afternoon
    I saw you up the eucalyptus tree –
The tree you said you really had to prune –
    And you were never one to let things be!
The lawn below with branches was bestrewn.
    And this was to your character the key:

You're practical (you handle shears with skill)
    And energetic (all the time hands-on),
Determined to succeed (you have the will)
    And brave: although your arm has undergone
Many an operation, you are still
    The girl whose face among the branches shone.

I saw it first that far Darjeeling day -
    The quality that's lasted down the years:
Such fixity of purpose does not stray,
    Such fortitude inspires and endears.
Thus can a photo truthfully portray
    The loved one up a gum tree with her shears!

Summer, 2002 ✍

TO HILARY

Our dear friend Hilary Brand died suddenly in her brother's London garden, after picking soft fruit (she was a great jam maker). It happened to be the tenth anniversary of the London bombings, when two minutes' silence was observed across the land. A physiotherapist by profession, she was also a talented musician and sportswoman. Her death came shockingly, without warning. Her body lay there in the tree's shade for the rest of the day. This poem was used at her funeral.

You left us – all too suddenly, too soon.
    The fruit was ripe for picking, so you went
To pick – and to be picked – at day's high noon,
    A life so fully lived, too swiftly spent.

The fruit was gathered in, the job was done.
    In the tree-filtered sunshine there you lay,
Your music silenced and your last game won –
    And somehow, for us all, 'twas close of play.

You chose to go (or, rather, you were chosen)
    While London mourned the blood the bombers shed;
At noon business suspended, action frozen,
    Two minutes' hush, for limbs and hearts that bled.

But you, through whose skilled hands pain found relief,
    Whose tender, practised touch made bodies strong,
Cannot now quickly cure us of our grief:
    To you our love and gratitude belong.

We loved you for your spirit and your drive;
    Though small of frame you always did walk tall,
And in our hearts your presence will survive,
Forever in our memory alive.
    The fruit is harvested. "Ripeness is all."

"Men must endure their going hence, even as their coming hither…
Ripeness is all." ('King Lear'}

In Thanksgiving

Hilary Christine Brand, née Rivers
2 November 1944 - 7 July 2015

Holy Trinity Church, Bengeo
Wednesday 29 July 2015
2.00pm

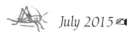 *July 2015*

TO MOTHER TERESA

who was recently canonized by Pope Francis. (Her Home for the Dying stands next door to the Temple of Kali, the Hindu Goddess of Destruction, awash daily with the blood of sacrificial goats. A startling juxtaposition!) Judy and I were privileged to meet her while doing our voluntary work in India, when she gave us her 'business card'.

Dear Mother Saint Teresa of Calcutta,
You worked more miracles than faith can utter.
Barefoot you went, diminutively small,
And yet among earth's titans you walked tall.

Goodness you saw in lives forever scarred
And beauty in the mangled and the marred.
You reached out to the leprous, the unwashed,
Embraced deformities, sought out the lost.

You trod the filth-strewn pavements of Calcutta
And looked to see God's glory in the gutter.
With Kali's bloody temple rituals vying,
You nursed the sick, brought comfort to the dying.

You recognized no chains of creed or caste,
You touched Untouchables, your love was vast.
You showed us there is good in all that breathes,
You taught us that by giving one receives.

The shame is ours: these things we also saw
But YOU glimpsed, in the poorest of the poor,
The face of Christ – on whom we shut the door.

October 2016

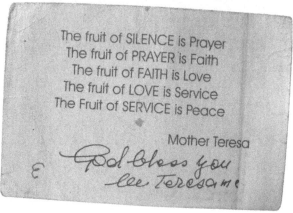

The fruit of SILENCE is Prayer
The fruit of PRAYER is Faith
The fruit of FAITH is Love
The fruit of LOVE is Service
The Fruit of SERVICE is Peace

Mother Teresa

God bless you
lee Teresa m

Mother Teresa's signed 'business card'

6

THINGS
THEY SAY

"ABSOLUTELY!"

A protest against the too frequent use of "absolutely".

What future is there for the small word "yes"
When many speakers favour "absolutely"
(Though needlessly emphatic, often heard,
Given much stress and uttered resolutely}?

Now "yes" is plain and simple, just one syllable.
Replaced by FOUR, it speaks too convolutely,
Lends too much weight to what is really trivial,
Offends the ear, can even hurt acutely.

No, "yes" is best: this is beyond dispute.
I totally reject (to put it crudely)
This poor polysyllabic substitute.
"Agree?" I ask. You answer "Absolutely!"!

August 2016 ✍

"UNACCEPTABLE"

"It's unacceptable!" they'll say –
 Emphatic, clear and strong!
Yet, somehow, after due delay,
 Things seem not quite so wrong:
The urge to action falls away
And brave convictions start to fray
('What good can it do, anyway?')
 And difficulties throng.
And thus the "unacceptable"
 Is accepted all along!

July 2017 ✍

"I KNOW WHERE YOU'RE COMING FROM"

"I know where you're coming from" some people say.
     Mysterious!! How can that be?
Do they mean "You've been shopping at Tesco's today"?
     Or "Your birthplace was Bexhill-on-Sea"?

Or are they just saying that they know me too well,
     Know me better than I know myself?
In which case I've nothing to show or to tell –
     I might as well stay on the shelf.

"I hear what you're saying." This, too, can annoy
     Since I fancy my voice loud and clear.
Or is it, perhaps, an ingenious ploy
     To prove that they have a good ear?

"I hear what you're saying and I know where you're coming from" –
     How clever! How clear and all-knowing!
(If only I, too, knew the road that I travel on! -
     But Heaven knows WHERE I am going!)

May 2017

"BLAH-BLAH-BLAH"

(I have always wanted to bring Kandahar into a poem: it's a lovely name.)

There is one phrase I would erase
    From here to Kandahar:
I do not like the current craze
    For saying "blah-blah-blah".
"Nonsense" is what this word conveys –
    We need not go too far
To find there are some better ways
    (A Black Sheep goes "Baa Baa").

"Gobbledegook" is a better word,
    Though somewhat la-di-da,
While "bosh" and "balderdash" I've heard
    And "crap" (which goes too far),
And "rhubarb rhubarb" is preferred
    On stage by many a star.
But most annoying and most absurd
    Is surely "blah-blah-blah".

Tis true that many a song we sing
    May well go "tra-la-la";
When caution to the winds we fling,
    We dance the cha-cha-cha -
And when we laugh at anything
    We bellow "ha ha ha!".
But none has a more hollow ring
    Than when we "blah-blah-blah".

And oftentimes our fond goodbyes
    Are childishly "ta-ta".
Expressing triumph or surprise,
    "Aha!!" we say, "Aha!!".
But circumstances may arise
    Wherein (it's quite bizarre)
Our psychobabble takes the prize,
    We just go "blah-blah-blah,
Blah-blah, blah-blah, blah-blah!"

September 2015 🖎

"NOT GETTING ANY YOUNGER"

(A particularly irritating euphemism)

'Not getting any younger' is a phrase quite often heard.
Though kindly meant and gently said, the wording is absurd!
Circumlocutions cannot hide the clear unvarnished truth:
'Not getting any younger' means 'you're too long in the tooth'.

'Not getting any younger' means 'becoming really old';
'Not getting any stronger ' means 'beginning to lose hold'.
'Not getting any slimmer' is a waistline that expands,
'Not getting any nimbler' when we've got arthritic hands,

'Not getting any fitter ' when we're often out of breath,
'Not getting any sharper' means we're nearly blind and deaf,
'Not getting any taller' when we find we've shrunk a lot,
'Not getting any brighter' when it's clear we've lost the plot.

'Not getting any younger.' Yes, the logic's not in doubt! -
And yet such blatant euphemisms we can do without.
Perhaps it's better just to say exactly what you mean:
'Good luck, my friend, you've had your day, it's time to quit
                                        the scene!'

August 2017

"END OF"

Some folk there are who make it their life's mission
    To tell us it's a sin as black as soot
To end a sentence with a preposition:
  It's something up with which they will not put.

But we who have more sense long since decided
    That pedantry like this we are no friend of;
Such prejudice is pointless and misguided –
  In fact, we say, it's utter nonsense. END of!

June 2017

"AT THE END OF THE DAY"

(A pox on clichés!)   *February 2011*

"At the end of the day" is what people say
In a cliché-bound state of paralysis;
If this you would shun, say "When all's said and done"
Or else "In the final analysis".

"In the light of eternity" means much the same –
And for classical scholars the art is
To say it in Latin, from which it first came:
"Sub specie aeternitatis."

Such distinctions we draw, at day's end - or before -
"In the long run" are quite unimportant;;
"At the end of the day" is too easy to say,
So we say it – though really we oughtn't!

At the end of the day, work is followed by play,
Then a nightcap – the evening's highlight.
It's the time of the day that we hold very dear.
No metaphor here! It's abundantly clear
It means slippers and fireside and twilight!

"ENJOY!"

"Enjoy!" you say – a kindly thought indeed,
    Although to grammar most insensitive,
Since dictionaries are generally agreed
    This is a verb that cannot be intransitive.

What is it that you tell me to enjoy?
    In vain I wait to hear the object follow:
    Enjoy my meal? Enjoy myself?
    Enjoy the day? Enjoy good health?
    Enjoy whatever I hear? or see? or swallow?
"Enjoy" must always have a word to follow!

To whatsoever "enjoy" may here allude
(Whether my health or wealth or self or food),
It's clearly meant to elevate my mood.
I must not, therefore, let the word annoy:
Rather, a ready smile I will deploy
    Whenever someone says to me "Enjoy!"

A word to follow?
No – just let it drop!
And learn to say "Enjoy!"
That's all.
Full stop.

April 2012 ✍

"HI, GUYS!"

(A pedantic protest against this increasingly common, gender-blind greeting)

Since Eve was made from Adam's rib
We've come some way via Women's Lib:
We're equal now – so no surprise
That boys and girls are all called "guys"!

Yet HE's a guy and SHE's a doll
(Or, if you like, she's someone's moll) –
But I have other fish to fry:
I'm NOT a doll, I am a guy.

That we are different none denies –
Why, then, the need for this disguise?
Gunpowder Plot? No mystery stalks! –
The culprit was a Guy - called Fawkes.

A man's a "fellow", "chap" or "bloke"
And people can be known as "folk" –
But SHE's a woman, "lady", "lass":
To make her masculine is crass.

Being called a "guy" could well offend her,
Suggesting she might be transgender.
Sex is ignored, I know not why:
However often she may try,
A WOMAN'S CLEARLY NOT A GUY!

(And I should tell you, by the by,
I'd rather not be greeted "Hi!".)

June 2016

"CAN'T COMPLAIN!"

Whatever may go wrong for us,
    However great our pain,
Whenever life is hard on us
We like our friends to think of us
    As patient – "Can't complain!"

And when one asks us how things go,
    Then, rather than explain
Or tell our troubles blow by blow
Or let our hidden weakness show –
    We just say "Can't complain!"

And even when, sound as a bell
    And feeling right as rain,
And all is going really well,
At understatement we excel:
    "Not too bad - can't complain!"

July 2016

"I'M FINE"

They say "How are you?"
Do they really wish to know?
We reply "Fine, thanks."
Do we mean it?
Or we might say "Not too bad, thanks. Can't complain."
Our reluctance to complain, of course, lets them off the hook.
But they might say "That's a qualified answer. What would you
    complain about if you could?"
We might then retreat and say again "No, really, I'm fine."
Or else we might seize the moment:
 "Actually, since you ask me, I've got a heavy cold and I'm not
sleeping well and my ingrowing toenail is hurting me and the
dentist says I have tooth decay and I have various aches and
I am plagued by doubts about the future and I'm acutely aware
of my own mortality and I'm worried about my investments .
and about the leak in the roof which I can't locate.
But thank you for asking."

Well, of course, we all have these things. Mustn't complain!
At least we have our life, for a little longer.
"Fine" is a weasel word.
With regard to the weather, 'fine" can mean "cloudless"
    or else merely "not wet".
Or it can be sarcastic: "That's a fine thing to say!"
Or again, "That's all very fine but…" means that it's not fine at all.
Your 'finery" could be your best bib and tucker (all fine and dandy)
–

Or else it could be your hand-me-downs, your tatters,
  your nakedness.
"I'm fine" often means "Don't ask me, please, leave me alone,
I've no wish to expose myself and my frailty. I'm fine."
("How are you?" is too searching, too precise – though "I'm fine"
  can still fob it off.)

"How do you do" is, by contrast, undemanding
  (as well as somewhat highfalutin).
It requires no response except for its repetition by the other
  party – the same question tossed neatly back:
"How do you do."… "How do you do."
Ball in your court!
There are no question marks here.
The surface civility begs the question.
No need to probe, no need to register the tone of voice,
No need even to hear it..
"How do you do" is not much more than a polite clearing
  of the throat

But "How are you?" is the most frequent enquiry. .
"I'm fine" is the hoped-for, expected answer
  and is gratefully accepted..
Honour is satisfied.
There can then follow a smooth transition to a topic such as
  the weather.

By such devices are the world's wheels kept oiled.

January 2016 ✍

123

"I'M GOOD"

"How Are you?" Thus the well-known greeting goes:
    The answer, like as not, is "I am good" -
But many a problem this reply can pose,
    The word is readily misunderstood.

Either the speaker sees himself as glorious,
    Successfully pursuing his career –
Or else he means that he is meritorious,
    Choosing the moral high ground as his sphere.

"Good" is a word that may be hagiographic,
    Connoting saintly figures robed in white,
Calling to mind "cherubic" and "seraphic"
    Like angels and archangels in full flight.

Now "good" can also mean idealistic
    And always doing all the things one should –
But self-assessment should be more realistic:
    Can ANYBODY truly be THAT good?

Goodness is not to everybody's taste
    And ethics can too easily encroach:
"I'm good, I'm blameless, virginal and chaste –
    In short, I really am beyond reproach!"

No! "Good" in this regard means "well and healthy"
    And nothing virtuous is understood –
Not necessarily well behaved or wealthy
(Though these are things I would be if I could).

    You kindly ask me how I am? I'm good!

"WITH GREAT RESPECT"

(which usually means 'with no respect at all')

I hear your words but – with respect –
    I cannot quite agree;
And I must say – with great respect –
    Your point I fail to see.
The fact is – with all due respect
    (If I may be so bold) –
You've got it wrong (no disrespect!)
    And I the truth uphold.

With huge respect, you're incorrect
    (If I may be so rash).
I'll tell you straight, I'll be direct:
    Your argument is trash,
Your data-base you have not checked,
Your views I totally reject,
I've never heard (with GREAT respect)
    Such utter BALDERDASH!

August 2017

"LIKE"

There are those who pepper their talk liberally with "like".
They say "I was, like, surprised, like!"
An admissible attempt at comparison, no doubt –
but WHAT is being compared with WHAT?
It is hard to say.
"I was, like, surprised". Not ACTUALLY surprised, it seems -
but LIKE surprised! How like?
Taken aback, perhaps? Or astonished? or astounded?
Or shocked? Or thunderstruck, indeed?
There is a conspicuous lack of precision.

There is more to it than this:
The over-use of "like" tends to render all experience merely virtual.
It suggests a fragile contract with reality, an unconsummated
    relationship with the real world:
Everything is analogous. Everything is like something else.
Like it or not, we are bombarded with vain comparisons.

But, of course! I now understand:
"Like" has become simply a form of punctuation, along with
    commas and semi-colons.
Like I said, I was, like, on the verge of, like, making a mistake.
So repeated "like"s indicate, if not a passion for comparisons,
    then a certain paucity of vocabulary.
"I was, like, WOW!"

I have a confession to make:
There are (like) certain things (like) that I don't (like) LIKE.
Like most of this poem, for example.
And I (like) like "like" like a hole in the head.
Do I, like, make myself, clear? I trust you are like-minded?

'I TELL A LIE'

(I should not let this rather silly phrase irritate me as much as it does!)

"I tell a lie."
"No, you do not. You have NOT just lied: you have merely
    made a mistake, a small factual error – which you are
    about to correct.
A lie is an intentional deception, a distortion or subversion
    of the truth!
There was no mendacity in your small piece of misinformation
    (which, anyway, you are about to correct).
It was an entirely innocent aberration.

Alas! The rest of us do, at times, lie.
You, too, probably lie on other occasions.
Mankind is given to lying – usually without admitting to it,
    such is the human tendency to deceive in one's own
    interests.
But in THIS instance you have not lied!

The honesty of what you say here is palpable.
On this particular occasion (untypically, maybe) you are clearly
    not culpable. Your motives are as pure as driven snow.
Do NOT, therefore, resort to a bogus confession of mendacity.
Simply say (which may be harder!) 'I've made a mistake'.
We shall then, of course, forgive you the slight inaccuracy –
    which in any case you were about to correct.
That was no lie!
End of!

September 2017

"TO BE QUITE HONEST"

"To be quite honest" people say,
    Which comes as some surprise!
A candid claim, I have no doubt –
    And yet the phrase implies
That everything they said till now
    Was just a pack of lies.

"I'll be quite honest with you" – Ah!
    Thank God for such veracity!
To take on board another fraud
    Is outside my capacity;
Here's truth indeed! a welcome break
    From brazen-faced mendacity.

And yet - to be quite honest with you -
    Now I'm not so sure
That I can trust implicitly
    Such candour any more:
Those claims to be so squeaky clean!
    Was there no truth before?

July 2017

"ONE OF THOSE THINGS"

What can we say about outrageous fortune?
    How best describe its arrows and its slings?
Often, of course, we label it 'misfortune' -
    Or else we say it's "just one of those things".

Battlers and athletes, men of all conditions,
    Throwing their gauntlets into many rings
And failing to achieve their brave ambitions,
    Will sadly smile – "It's just one of those things."

What can we blame for this or that disaster?
    We do not know who really pulls the strings.
While Fortune's fickle wheel spins ever faster
    We shrug it off as: "just one of those things!"

If someone COULD explain to honest doubters
    The rise and fall of emperors and kings
And all the mysteries of the world about us
And all the laws that operate without us –
    We'd still say, with a sigh, "It's one of those things"!

August 2012 (after the London Olympics)

129

"SO"

I have enough material to write a new polemic:
    It's all about that irritating "so".
Starting a sentence with a "so" is now an epidemic.
    A weasel word, I wish that it would go!

"So" as an introductory word is vague as any vapour –
    So what? It is a word with many missions:
But here it's little more than conversational wallpaper
    Or a clever tactic used by politicians.

So many "so"s we often use, it's easy to recite 'em,
    So use 'em if you wish, go with the flow:
So far so good! so be it! and so on, ad infinitum –
    But please don't START a sentence with a "so"!
    It's just about as low as you can go.

July 2016

"SO WHAT?!"

"So what?!"
Can there be any rejoinder more dismissive, more defiant,
    more arrogant?
Can there be any more effective conversation-stopper`.

"So what?!" will pierce any armour, prick any bubble, crush
    any opposition.
It is a monumental put-down, a knock-out blow.
It deflates the ego, it lays pretension bare.

"So what" rhymes with insulting names like "clot", "sot" and "blot
    on the horizon".
It rhymes, too, with the small and insignificant: "dot", "spot", "tot"
    and "I don't care a jot".

It can puncture a cliché:
"A garden is a lovesome thing, God wot". "So what?!"
It terminates all argument: "That's the lot!"
It silences the other person – like a garotte.

It demands to be doubly punctuated, being both a question
    and an exclamation:
"So what?" "So what!" –
Contemptuous query and brutal rebuttal at the same time.

I trust that I have exposed this unpleasant expression for what it is?
You are at liberty, of course, to reply
"SO WHAT?!"

May 2016 ✍

"STOOD" OR "SAT"

Since I'm the pedant always fit for branding –
    There's one phrase I would banish if I could:
Instead of saying, correctly, "I was standing"
    Some will insist on saying "I was STOOD".

Such vile abuse of verbs is unremitting.
    "I'm stood" is bad – and, even worse than that,
Instead of (quite correctly) "I was sitting",
    Unblushing, they will tell you "I was SAT"!

No doubt you'll say that I am being pedantic –
    'Tis true, I can't deny it under oath:
Such infelicities do send me frantic -
But I must learn to tolerate this antic
    Wherever I am 'STOOD' or 'SAT' – or both.

February 2015

"IF ANYTHING HAPPENED..."

(Another tiresome euphemism)

"If anything happened to me" people say,
    Or 'if anything happened to you…"
But of course things are happening every day –
    And usually out of the blue.

"If anything happened" – there's so much could happen!
    Things happen each hour that goes by!
I might well be rained upon, snowed upon, sat upon,
    I might freak, I might freeze, I might fry.

I might well be asked to the Palace, indeed,
    To talk with the Queen and take tea.
 I might have been cited and possibly knighted –
    These are things that might happen to me.
    It depends on the Powers that Be.

And "anything" could well be any old thing!
    Things happen– so why all the fuss?
"IF ANYTHING HAPPENED TO YOU, MY DEAR…"
Yes, I know what you're trying to say, my dear,
(In practice your meaning is perfectly clear):
    IF I SHOULD RUN UNDER A BUS!

August 2017 ✍

"TAKE CARE!"

(A protest against the increasing use of "Take care!" as a parting shot)

"Take care!" we say – the phrase is trite,
    The words are anodyne,
A godless version of "goodbye",
    Well meant (no doubt), benign –
But, caution-bound, they show scant faith
    In Providence Divine.

"Goodbye!" is "God be with you!"
    But the substitute "Take care!",
Dismissing God's omnipotence,
    Suggests that He's elsewhere.
These words, however kindly meant,
    Can hardly be a prayer.

"Take care!" I'm told. How must I go?
    How fittingly respond?
How arm myself? A loaded gun?
    Ratsbane? A magic wand?
A panoply war-proof, maybe –
    And something more, beyond?

Take care of what? Dangers ahead,
    Of which I'm not aware?
A tiger in the street, perhaps?
    Infection in the air?
Or is it Armageddon - and
    A counsel of despair?

"Take care!" we say: a risk-aversion
    Culture is implied,
A nanny state grimly despotic,
    Caution nationwide
And carefree spontaneity
    Implicitly denied.

"Adieu!" is French, "Farewell!" too formal,
    Goes against the grain;
While "See you later, alligator"
    Is a poor refrain!
"So long!" and "Cheers!" are free and easy,
    Said in cheerful vein.
But best is "Goodbye!" – "God be with you
    Till we meet again!"

21st May 2012 ✍

"WOW!"

Among the words of wonderment which dictionaries allow,
There's one spontaneous little bleep, of just three letters – "**WOW!**".
This open-mouthed apostrophe, this breathless exclamation
Expresses much, from mild surprise to fervent admiration.

Now "**WOW!**" is inarticulate, a word more mouthed than spoken,
Yet says it all – a wide-eyed accolade it may betoken.
No need for lengthy eulogy, no call for fulsome praise,
This little palindrome will do – spelt just the same both ways.

Now "awesome" properly means "inspiring reverential fear",
While "stunning" only renders one unconscious, it is clear.
"Fantastic comes from "fantasy" – it's only in the mind –
Alternatives to "cool" and "brill" are difficult to find.

"To **WOW!**", "to woo" – it's all the same (a sweetheart understands)
And anyone whom you can **WOW** is putty in your hands.
And every critic knows, and every author, every actor,
That what the world is looking for is simply "the **WOW** factor".

To say all that we want to say - quite briefly - none knows how:
There is no word that's shorter or more meaningful than "**WOW!**"
No clearer recognition of some marvel in its prime,
No better way to capture the ineffably sublime.

And when on Darien's peak stout Cortez* stood,
                              with all his men
Reduced to silence by the sight of seas beyond their ken,
It's possible that someone DID speak up and so endow
Our language with a brave new word – "There's the Pacific – **WOW!**"

In fief to our astonishment, we know not what to say
But to our lips that little word comes pat and straight away.
Some have a winning way with words: to these, of course, we bow;
It would be great to articulate – if only one knew how.
But on the whole, when wonderstruck, we utter, simply,
                              WOW!"

"**WOW!**

*(See Keats's sonnet 'On First Looking into Chapman's Homer':
    "Or like stout Cortez when, with eagle eyes
    He stared at the Pacific – and all his men
    Looked at each other with a wild surmise –
    Silent – upon a peak in Darien.")*

August 2014

7

HAPPENSTANCES

❖

ACCIDENT

On Easter Day 2016 Judy fell while playing table-tennis in a barn with a concrete floor. She fractured her pelvis and was immobilized for some weeks.

We cannot know what lies in store.
    That which we thought a game
Proved unforgiving as a concrete floor.
    Out of the sky it came -

One small slip, a single fall.
    The life we call our own
Is lightweight as a ping pong ball,
    Brittle as pelvic bone,

Fragile as this Spring's windblown blossom,
    Like chestnut's splendid rig
Which buds, blooms, fades and turns to flotsam,
    Inconsequential as a twig.

Ping pong, a concrete floor, a stumble –
    By such we are brought low,
Made more aware, more whole, more humble
    That we in grace may grow,
Through weakness made more strong! 'Twas ever so.

May 2016

The drawing-room became the temporary bedroom at Bonners, Surrey

A MAN'S LEGS

(Lines written for a friend who was appalled at the prospect of losing her hair from chemotherapy). Psalm 147: 10,11 "The Lord taketh no pleasure in the legs of a man… (He) taketh pleasure in them that hope for His mercy."

Man's legs, says the Psalmist, give God no delight,
    Be they never so strong or so fair.
So it follows, as surely as day follows night,
    He's not too concerned about hair.

Legs weaken, and hair becomes scant, and the old
    Are accustomed to losing their teeth,
But the one thing we hold (we must hoard it like gold)
    Is the person we are, underneath!

When our strength and our hair and our teeth are all spent
    We can still praise the Lord at our leisure;
In hope and in faith we shall then be content,
    Knowing THIS is what gives the Lord pleasure.

20th October 2015

AS ONE DOES

I have always pursued the good life, preferring plenitude to poverty -
As one does.
Tomorrow I shall wake up to the sound of the live-in maid's
    light footstep on the stair.
I shall luxuriate under the duvet in anticipation of the Lapsang
    Souchong (with lemon) which will shortly arrive, along with the FT.
I shall order eggs and smoked salmon for breakfast –
    and perhaps some devilled kidneys -
And from my bed, before showering, I shall probably book
    a Caribbean cruise.
    As one does.

After breakfast I shall take a spin in my Bentley convertible
And enjoy a spoiling massage in my spa downstairs, followed
    by a restorative sauna.
I shall call my wealth manager for some clarification regarding
    my hedge funds.
I shall then lunch at Claridge's and spend the afternoon at the
    Club, sampling their latest vintage while watching the people
    get wet.
Later on I shall honour an obligation to dine with some friends
    at La Gavroche.
    As one does.

Tomorrow night it is possible that I shall not be here,
    unavoidably detained
Having suffered a massive cardiac arrest.
I shall then face the consequences of a largely wasted life.
    As one does.

AT SEA

In worthless things Mankind perversely chooses to invest
    Its blood and sweat and tears and eggs and sperm:
It scuffles to succeed, pursues its goals with fitful zest
    And manifestly lacks a purpose firm.

Beguiled we are by baubles, do not see the real thing,
    In ignorance we turn and turn about.
We strain after possessions and find dross to which to cling
    And faith long since gave way to chronic doubt.

We batten down the hatches, think to ride out every storm
    But - confusing port with starboard, right with left -
Inexorably towards the rocks our frail craft is drawn,
    Of moral compass patently bereft.

We scan the wide horizons – but of succour there is naught,
    In the offing there is nothing danger-free.
In spite of its contrivances to find the way to port
    Our troubled world is terribly at sea.

Although in dire straits Mankind seems helplessly to drift,
    On high seas rudderless to roam,
The skills of seamanship we lack are all in Heaven's gift,
    To navigate the fury and the foam:
Wisdom we need, and fortitude - and prayer which we may lift
    To the Pilot who can steer us safely home.

October 2016

I HAVE LOST MY SPRING

"'I've lost my spring" the old man said,
    While struggling from the sofa,
"And as for getting out of bed -
    You'd take me for a loafer."

I sympathized with him, of course,
    Not really comprehending:
Being young, I thought my own life force
    Would never have an ending.

But I have lost my spring long since,
    My summer, too, has gone,
My autumn's here, with all its tints,
    And winter's coming on.

Yet though stiff limbs and joints protest,
    Things are by no means over –
So long as I can keep abreast
Of that which makes this life so blest
And find again my youthful zest
    And get up off the sofa.

November 2015

DRESSING UP

One universal truth we must acknowledge:
A fashion show's as good as any college.
The catwalk sparkles with aspiring scholars –
A lady learns to look a million dollars.

We like to talk of life in terms of dressing
And clothing metaphors we find a blessing.
Thus, when a man is eloquent enough,
We say he makes his speeches "off the cuff";
Or if the mark he rashly overshoots,
'Tis clear this man is "too big for his boots".
As sure as hens lay eggs and cows are browsers,
'Tis certain there are wives who "wear the trousers".
And when a woman's age she tries to sham,
We know she's really "mutton dressed as lamb".

Our whole life is a garment to unravel:
From swaddling-clothes to winding-shroud we travel.
Deceptive the disguises that are worn –
The truth is, mother-naked we were born!
Moths will devour our clothes – a message stern –
From dust we came, to dust we shall return.
Yet many a popinjay leaves as memorial
His fancy for flamboyancy sartorial.
In dressing to the nines we take much pleasure –
Would that our lives, like clothes, were made to measure!

But when we're qualified to leave this place,
Quite stripped of all our finery and grace,
(Our bombazine, organza, muslin, lace
And all our wardrobe vanished without trace) –
We'll meet the Grand Designer face to face!

June, 2015

IT'S NOT THE WINNING,
IT'S THE TAKING PART

*Composed at Bishop Cotton School, Simla, and used in the School Chapel,
on the day of the School's cross country run.*

There are those who have the strength, there are those who
have the speed,
There are those who have a racing start;
But the judges in the race of life are all agreed
It's not the winning, it's the taking part.

There are prizes to compete for - medals silver, bronze and gold -
There are trophies for the talented and smart,
But the race is to the stayer (if the real truth be told):
It's not the winning, it's the taking part!

There are those born to be clever, winning scholarly awards,
There are praises, too, for every skill and art;
But the giving of your level best will bring its own rewards –
It's not the winning, it's the taking part.

And when they add the scores up and the figures start to mount,
They will mark you high for never losing heart!
There are credits, there are debits, sure! – but in the final count
It's not the winning, it's the taking part.

March 1999

Justin runs the London Marathon, 1997

LITTER

Our throw-away society!
    The scum swills round our feet,
The tatters of propriety
    Are blown across the street.
Our legacy, quite simply,
    Is the trash which we excrete.

Sit lightly to this littered world
    In its pollution drowned!
The toys which from our pram we hurled
    Lie broken on the ground
And Mammon's flags, by us unfurled,
    Are billowing all around.

And when the end has come to pass
    On what shall souls then feed?
Will concrete cover all the grass?
    Will forests be un-treed?
And when we tread on broken glass
    Will calloused feet still bleed?

In trumpery our trust is placed,
    Its pleasures run to seed.
With vision blurred, with blunted taste,
With hoarded coinage soon debased,
Wearied, we wallow in our waste,
    Bankrupted by our greed.

And yet – renewal will come, my friend,
    To this so ravaged scene:
Earth's increase will itself defend,
    Its streams again run clean,
Its broken bones will surely mend,
Its birdsong never shall have end,
From scorched earth there will spring, my friend,
    Fresh shoots of living green.

May 2016

MATUTINAL

The confessions of an early riser.

Early morning is a time of maximum availability.
The mind is uncluttered, the clock ticks unemphatically.
The day, not yet smudged by happenings or doings,
         is available for inaction and contemplation.
It is quiet as a nun.

Early morning is a country without borders, entered
                              without passport,
accessible to denizens and foreigners alike.
It is a land to be passed through without let or hindrance.
It is free.

Early morning is when we can still recall the details
                         of Yesterday
before receiving the mandatory palimpsest of Today
         with its crowded canvas of events and encounters.
Yesterday's experience, though fast fading, is still available.

Early morning makes available a world of the imagination
         and holds the promise of freedom.
It supplies the blank sheet and fuels the pen with ink.
It sharpens the mind's focus.
It empowers the spirit.

It is also the one time, perhaps,
                 when I am available to myself.

October 2016

HEALTH AND SAFETY

Good HEALTH is something nobody
  would rather be without!
And SAFETY means security –
  a boon, we do not doubt!
But when they're yoked together,
  very neatly juxtaposed,
We pursue them hell for leather
  with our minds completely closed!

To be a stalwart race we can
  no longer make pretence:
It's clear that 'Health & Safety'
  leaves no room for commonsense.
(It's now too dangerous, we're told,
  to play a game of conkers –
Which shows you that our nation bold
  has gone completely bonkers.)

Britannia once did rule the waves.
  The seas we used to straddle
Are now proclaimed a health risk
  And it's dangerous to paddle.
And thus our freedoms, one by one,
  are filched from us by stealth,
Till, wrapped in cotton wool, we're safe and sound –
  AND ON THE SHELF!

July 2017✍

MEASURE FOR MEASURE

He was a banker and consequently in the business
                                of measuring.
He measured meticulously his gains and losses and
                                believed in market economics.
At work his approach was always measured,
                                with a shrewd eye to profit.
His hedge funds were seen as an almost safe bet
And even his gambles were an investment.
'Investment' was his favourite word:
His wife, his family, his friendships were all an investment,
                                the risks carefully measured;
With expert eye he took the measure of his clients –
                                and played golf with them;
He was ahead of the game, by a long measure.
He measured his assets at leisure: his yacht measured
    64 feet, his cellar measured many vintages;
His suits, his cars, his properties were made to measure.
Just as carefully he measured his chances in love,
                                in marriage, in life.
His opinions were measured, in accordance with the
    company he happened to be in.
He could afford a lifestyle congenial beyond measure
And he slept in measureless content.

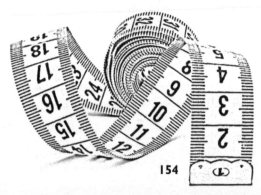

154

But he overlooked the truth that a chain's weakest link
                              is the measure of its strength:
At the end, after a good dinner, he measured his length
                              on the floor,
At which point his severance package was forfeit.
He was then measured for his coffin.
At the same time he was measured for his eligibility for
     the Kingdom – with a negative finding.
Moreover, he was weighed in the balances and found wanting.
You could say that Someone had the measure of him!

October 2014 ✍

NEIGHBOURS

Our near neighbour Les died, suddenly and without warning,
of a massive stroke.

We hadn't seen Les recently,
     "You must come round" we said,
"Next week, perhaps…" Thus, carelessly,
     Our separate lives we led.

God make us be more neighbourly
     Since life hangs by a thread!
That social call was not to be –
     By next week Les was dead.

25th September 2017 ✍

MR P

I know a man called Parkinson
    (I call him Mr P),
His hand shake is a giveaway –
    He sometimes spills the tea.

He's full of good intentions, but
    He lacks get-up-and-go;
He'd like to move more smartly, but
    His feet make him go slow.

He'd like to take life in his stride
    With ease that none could ruffle –
But I have noticed, on the side,
    His stride becomes a shuffle.

Left to himself, without the pills
    He might be a no-hoper –
But there's a cure for all his ills,
    Her name is Carol Doper*.

If Carol can indeed contrive
    To be his daily dosage,
He knows that he will then survive
    At least into his dotage.

Now Mr P is keen, of course,
    To use his modest talents
But there are times when he, perforce,
    Loses his sense of balance.

To be quite honest, if I'm pressed
    To name this Mr P,
It is (as you by now have guessed)
    Another name for ME.

Degenerate, Regenerate –
    Two words almost the same
Except for one small letter, which
    Can really change the game.

And so I am regenerated,
    Seeing all life afresh:
I find my spirit (thank the Lord!)
    Is stronger than the flesh.

A hand shake, leg shake, any shake,
    Whatever shake it be,
(A question now of make or break)
I know the steps that I must take,
However much my limbs may quake –
    I'm friends with Mr P!

*Careldopa is the essential prescribed medication

February 2016

 = *Breakfast*

RHYME

Much great poetry is non-rhyming. I like writing it myself. However…

It has been proved a thousand times,
That people like a poem that rhymes -
In fact, some say, it is a crime
To avoid a nice, mouth-filling rhyme,
They cannot tolerate for a minute
A poem that has no rhyming in it.
They say that a good clinching rhyme
Is so mellifluous, so sublime
That it approaches the divine
(Though, strictly, that is not a rhyme).

You'll find few things more satisfying,
Than rhyming when you're versifying:
You'll find (in case you didn't know it)
That you are an accomplished poet.
You'll find out that it's not so hard
To make a rhyme and be a bard.
A rhyme is just a verbal mime,
It mimics sounds, it keeps the time,
Euphonious as a church bell's chime –
Of elegance a paradigm!

But just in case you think that I'm
A master of the art of rhyme –
At times my rhyme's too close to call,
Technically not a rhyme at all,
Like saying that the sun is shining
And making "shining" rhyme with "rhyming" -
Far from being a verbal feat
It's really a poetic cheat.

With rhyming we have much affinity,
Find it the ultimate concinnity,
And so there is no rhyme or reason
(Indeed, it could be seen as treason)
Not to employ this simple trick
Which gives one's readers such a kick.
'Gainst nature 'tis a monstrous crime
(An Aussie would say a "grite shime")
If any poet in his prime
Should ever fail, at any time,
To use a good, mouth-filling …
                    …identity of sound between words.

September 2016

THE WEATHER

How is it that when two or three
    Are gathered all together,
They only really feel free
    To talk about the weather?

"Last week was chilly", one will say,
    "This week, so far, is wetter...
It rained a little yesterday,
    Tomorrow may be better."

If in the street a friend we meet,
    Then all we need to say
- In rain or mist or snow or sleet,
When winter gales blow a treat
And floods are rising round our feet -
    Is "Not so nice today!"

    When stuck for something new to say,
    We're all birds of a feather:
To keep embarrassment at bay -
No awkward silence in the way -
    We talk about the weather.

Forget Assad, Islam and ISIS
   And Europe's state of flux.
A useful way to break the ice is
To talk about the REAL crisis –
    "Nice weather for the ducks!"

To ban all topics that might vex
    Is always our endeavour:
No politics, religion, sex –
We change the subject, clear the decks
    And talk about the weather.

Of other topics there are stacks:
    Iraq, Iran, whatever…
The migrant problem, credit tax,
The economy, the fiscal cracks
And cybercrime (are laws too lax?)
How Brexit wrecks it, puts up backs,
Fifa, corruption, facing facts,
Drug cheaters on Olympic tracks
And refugees who live in shacks
And child-abuse, the sordid facts
    And heads we ought to sever,
The House of Lords, and Goldman Sachs,
Chilcott Enquiry - what it lacks,
The N.H.S. (where falls the axe?)
Hacking – and how a hacker hacks,
Fracking –and why a fracker fracks,
    And Putin, who's so clever -
And yet we cover all our tracks
And on such trivia turn our backs
    And talk about the weather.

Now here's a tip: if you have reached
    The far end of your tether,
If you have lost the will to live,
If you have nothing left to give
    And no joy whatsoever,
Forget about the daily grind,
Remember this: you're sure to find
That everyone's immensely kind –
(Indeed, you will be wined and dined)
    They'll think you rather clever -
So long as you are well resigned
To give up thinking, close your mind
    And talk about the weather.

December 2015

IN TRANSIT

(written at Nairobi Airport – or what remained of it after the fire in October 2013 – en route from Zimbabwe to London)

It's Tannoy Testing – one, two, three, four, five" –
    Nairobi Airport – nine more hours to wait!
"Jambo!" The speaker system comes alive,
    The heat lies heavy as unwanted freight.
Again the 'Tannoy Testing' system's on,
    The human traffic goes its various ways.
No soul has respite till the waiting's done,
    The transit hall went up in last week's blaze.

Close to Gate 7 I now take up my station,
    A piece of flotsam borne towards the shore,
For this is not my final destination –
    I am a soul in transit evermore.
A form to fill for ticking every box –
    Time hangs still heavier – five more hours to go –
And do they tick, those slow demented clocks?
    Is there a Heaven? and is it called Heathrow?

Heavy the weight of many hours' duration,
    Heavy my baggage, safe (I hope) in hold –
But this is not my final destination.
    Now as a Kenyan refugee enrolled,
The flight to freedom's worth the wait, I'm told.

And this is where I must, I shall, I CAN sit
For ever - foreordained to be in transit. ✈ ✈ ✈ ✈

EIGHTY (80)

80 has crept up on me –
    I never thought it would!
I always thought that three-score years
    And ten were understood.

But now that I'm aware that I
    Have lived on borrowed time –
I'll seize the opportunity
    To pen another rhyme!

23rd January 2105 ✍

FOURSCORE!

It's eighty years, I'm told, beyond all reasonable doubt,
Since I did make my inconspicuous entry;
Which means, as mathematics make it easy to work out,
    I've been around for four-fifths of a century.

No longer a grammarian or stuffy antiquarian,
    All caution to the winds I now have flung,
No one, I trust, will label me a valetudinarian -
But I can boast of being a new octogenarian -
    The word rolls very sweetly off the tongue.

In Sussex I was born, they say, in 1935
    When George the Fifth was King (to deal factually);
My passport clearly tells me I elected to arrive
    In Brighton, by the sea (well, Hove actually).

I grew up in the shadow of the rolling Sussex Downs –
    On which my wife is apt to pour much scorn:
She will refer to them (in passing) as "those bumps
                                        and mounds" –
    For she, of course, was Himalayan-born.

My prep school was evacuated down to craggy Devon,
    Which proved to be a blessing in disguise:
Running wild on those beetling cliffs was our idea of Heaven –
        Most of the staff, we judged, were German spies.

My 80th Birthday
canvas montage from Justin

My Marlborough, Army, Cambridge days came as a blessed
                                                            boon –
  Then teaching, in a quantity of places:
Merchiston, Falcon, Wrekin, Charterhouse, Haileybury, Doon –
  All schools which my career somehow embraces.

One place in India I did find especially appealing
  As, full of zest across the world I travelled –
The best view (as I very soon found out) was in Darjeeling –
  And THAT is where my bachelorhood unravelled.☞

At dating women, to be honest, I was not the cleverest –
    But Fortune intervened and changed my life:
With Judy, one cold morning, watching sunrise on Mount Everest,
    It dawned on me that I had found my wife!

Now Justin and Antonia were Bulawayo-born –
    White Africans, in tropic sunshine clad –
Until reluctantly to England's grey skies we were drawn
    And Bruno, therefore, is a Shropshire lad,

Now in this rambling chronicle of shameless country-hopping
    In many lands, with many a foreign visa,
I hope you'll kindly overlook a little quiet name-dropping –
    Yes, both of us have known - Mother Theresa!

And yes, I've witnessed in the flesh the near-immortal Elvis,
    As erogenous as everybody claims –
The throaty voice, the sultry smile and that gyrating pelvis –
    Girls screamed - his every movement fanned the flames.

From Kilimanjaro's summit I have viewed the vasty plains,
    Big Game I've seen on many a safari,
I've sailed from Durban to Japan to see the Olympic Games,
    I've hunted springbok in the Kalahari.

I've sailed into Sydney, seen the Opera House renowned,
    On Canada's trains I've worked, across the Rockies,
In the Dead Sea – unpleasantly – I very nearly drowned;
    High Newton's rather quieter than Bangkok is!

And now I've finally hung up my gown and mortar-board
    And cleared my lungs of all that blackboard chalk,
I see that there are many options still to be explored,
    I find I still (thank God!) can walk and talk!

And eighty's a good age to spread one's wings, to start exploring
    And not to be defeated by the Fells.
Even when gales are howling, mists descending,
                               rain downpouring,
The Lakes will never cease to weave their spells.

All beauty's here – becks burbling, lakes reflecting,
                           mountains soaring,
Daffs blooming, Herdwicks grazing – and, be sure,
                            there's no ignoring
    The clamorous peal of Cartmel Priory bells!

The poet Robert Browning has this message, wise and weighty:
    "Grow old," he says, "Grow old along with me."
And what is more, now that I've reached the youthful age of eighty
    I've Browning's word: "The best is yet to be!"

23rd January 2015 ✍

Above: Charterhouse School and
Left: Haileybury College prints
illustrated and designed
by Justin Hunt

ON WESTMINSTER BRIDGE

*On this day, 215 years after Wordsworth wrote his sonnet (opposite),
a radicalized Muslim brought terror to Westminster.*

Earth has not anything to show more dread!
Hard would he be of heart who could pass by
A sight so shocking in its travesty
Of all that's fair. The poet's calm has fled.
This City now doth, like a garment, shed
Its even tenor: men and women lie –
Along the Bridge and open to the sky –
At once struck down, the wounded and the dead!

Never did sun more cruelly lay bare
The dark dementia where two cultures meet.
Ne'er saw I, never smelt, more noisome air
Than rises from this carnage at my feet.
Dear God! it seems the very stones do stare
And all that mighty heart has ceased to beat.

22nd March 2017 ✎

Composed upon Westminster Bridge

Earth has not anything to show more fair:
Dull would he be of soul who could pass by
A sight so touching in its majesty;
This City now doth, like a garment, wear
The beauty of the morning: silent, bare,
Ships, towers, domes, theatres and temples lie
Open unto the fields and to the sky,
All bright and glittering in the smokeless air.

Never did sun more beautifully steep
In his first splendour, valley, rock or hill;
Ne'er saw I, never felt, a calm so deep!
The river glideth at his own sweet will:
Dear God! the very houses seem asleep
And all that mighty heart is lying still.

William Wordsworth, 31st July 1802

WE ♥ LDN

Show your solidarity
Our back page today is a poster to display your support for London in the face of terrorism

8

THE FAITH

❖

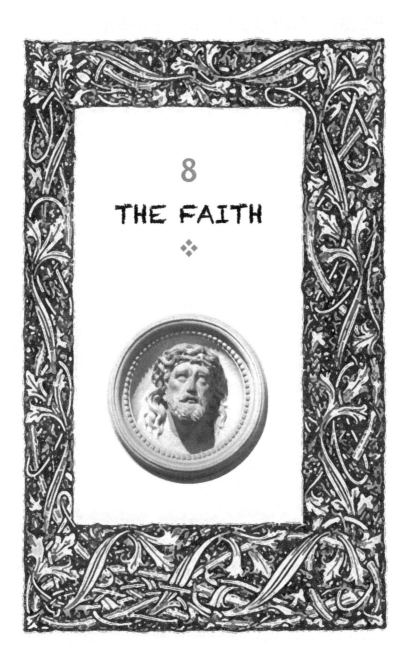

HYMN: CHRIST THE KING

Christ the King, our story,
    Christ the King, our song,
Christ in whom we glory,
    Christ for whom we long;
Christ the Lord around us,
    Christ the Lord above,
Christ whose grace is boundless,
    Christ whose name is Love.

Christ whose mercy meets us,
    Christ who pardons all,
Christ whose strength completes us,
    Christ who breaks our fall;
Christ who healed the suffering,
    Christ who raised the dead,
Christ Himself an offering,
    Christ the broken bread;

Christ whose death was for us,
    Christ who rose again,
Christ whose Light shines o'er us
    Evermore to reign.
God the eternal Father,
    God the living Son,
God the indwelling Spirit –
    Ever Three-in-One.

Words and music by David Hunt © Easter 2015

1. Christ the King, our story, Christ the King, our song,
2. Christ whose mercy meets us, Christ who pardons all,
3. Christ whose death was for us, Christ who rose again,

Christ in whom we glory, Christ for whom we long;
Christ whose strength completes us, Christ who breaks our fall;
Christ whose Light shines o'er us, Evermore to reign.

Christ the Lord around us, Christ the Lord above,
Christ who healed the suffering, Christ who raised the dead,
God th'eternal Father, God the living Son,

verses 1 & 2

Christ whose Grace is boundless, Christ whose name is Love.
Christ Himself an offering, Christ the broken bread;
God th'indwelling Spirit -

verse 3

Ever Three-in-One.

175

DOUBTING THOMAS

Thomas! Your name for doubting goes before you -
    Yet you have preached the Gospel near and far,
And many are the unbaptized who saw you
    In Persia, Babylon and Malabar.

Espousing India to the One-Begotten,
    Dispelling darkness with your brightest dawn,
Many you clad in robes of whitest cotton -
    These were your Christians, baptized and twice-born.

"I'll not believe it" once you said, still doubting,
    "Until I see the thing with my own eyes.
The laws of Nature were not made for flouting.
    You are deluded. Dead men do not rise!

"Except I see the very print of nails,
    Except I thrust my hand into His side,
I'll not forgive this greatest of betrayals:
    I thought the man immortal – and he died!"

Thomas, your lack of faith was an affliction,
    The sceptic's path defiantly you trod –
But then you saw the wounds: these were no fiction!
    "My Lord" you uttered, humbled, "and my God!"

So Thomas, we remember you, revere you,
    Of sceptics you remain the patron saint,
Your quest is ours, our doubting brings us near you,
    With you we seek for proof, our faith is faint.

But Christ said "Blest are those who, without seeing,
    Can yet believe". This is our sacred brief -
To pray, with every fibre of our being:
    "Lord, I believe: help Thou my unbelief!"

January 2016 ✍

St Thomas' Cathedral, Madras, India

GOD OUR PRESENT HELP IN TROUBLE *(Psalm 46)*

God, our present help in trouble,
God our strength, our refuge be.
Though the waters seethe in tumult,
Though earth surges like the sea,
Lo! The mountains and the ocean
Quake before God's majesty –
Therefore we'll not fear.

Lo! He snaps the spear in sunder,
Burns the chariot in the fire,
Heathens rage and kings are conquered:
God our stronghold stands entire!
God the lord of Hosts is with us,
Here to guide, protect, inspire –
Therefore we'll not fear.

See among the desolations
Mighty works of God displayed!
Hear His voice amid the tempest:
"Peace, 'tis I, be not afraid!"
Hail the Lord o'er earth exalted,
Honoured, worshipped and obeyed!
Therefore we'll not fear.

Words and music by David Hunt © January 2017

1. God, our pres - ent help in trou - ble. God, our strength, our re - fuge be. Though the wa - ters seethe in tu - mult, Though earth sur - ges like the sea. Lo! the moun - tains and the o - cean Quake be - fore God's ma - jes - ty There - fore we'll not fear.

2. Lo! He snaps the spear in sun - der, Burns the cha - riot in the fire, Hea - thens rage and kings are con - quered; God our strong - hold stands en - tire! God the Lord of Hosts is with us, Here to guide, pro - tect, in - spire There - fore we'll not fear.

3. See a - mong the de - so - la - tions Migh - ty works of God dis - played! Hear His voice a - mid the tem - pest, "Peace, 'tis I, be not a - fraid!" Hail the Lord o'er earth ex - al - ted, Hon - oured, wor - shipped and o - beyed! There - fore we'll not fear.

179

PRODIGAL

Down on his luck, and dinnerless,
    The son's shame was complete:
Reduced to looking after pigs,
    Forced to admit defeat,
He fain would fill his belly
    With the husks the swine did eat…

…Until a father's love stepped in
    To welcome and to heal,
To kill a fatted calf and make
    A celebratory meal:
Forgiveness unconditional –
    And a dish of tender veal.

A jealous elder brother
    Was the one dissenting voice,
To whom the father said "My son,
    We really have no choice:
Your brother who was lost is found –
    Good reason to rejoice!"

The story has a meaning clear:
    However low I sink,
A God who loves is close at hand
    To pull me from the brink,
Whose power to save me from myself
    Is greater than I think!

March 2017

MAKE NO MISTAKE!

Make no mistake, that Stable was no fable!
    'Twas true - the guiding Star none could deny.
Be sure, the Crucifixion was no fiction,
    Likewise the Resurrection was no lie.
The Ascension was by no means an invention:
    'Tis certain, on that day God did not die.
Kid yourself not! all this was God's intention.
Make no mistake! He'll be back by and by!

January 2017

MY GOD!

I am the God you said did not exist;
You are the child I loved – and always missed.

I am the God you kicked against and spurned;
Riches I gave you which you had not earned.

I am the God whose fault it was (you claimed}
That you were harshly judged, unfairly blamed.

I am the God you set out to dethrone:
"His own received Him not." – You were my own!

I am the God on whom you brought disgrace
That day when you denied me to my face.

I am the God by whom you lightly swore:
"My God!" you said – but it meant nothing more.

I am the God you still kept at arm's length,
Preferring to place faith in your own strength.

I am the God you hoped would disappear
When thought of judgement fed your guilty fear.

I am the God who did not care (you shouted),
The God who stood by while His laws were flouted.

I am the God who – when bereaved, you cried -
Was in the same place when my own Son died.

I am your God. That bond no man can sever,
In spite of all the world's malign endeavour,
And you, dear child, will be my child for ever.

March 2016

*Stone bust of the head of Christ
in Cartmel Priory, Cumbria*

GUILTY!

Guilty, m'lud, as charged!
    Too often, from my birth
When into your fair world I barged,
My vision fails to be enlarged
    By all the signs on earth
    Of God's so wondrous worth.

Guilty, my Lord, as charged!

August 2015

THE SINGER, NOT THE SONG

(No reference to any particular vicar may be inferred.)

You may not like the Vicar
  (You've a perfect right to hate him),
And his jokes may seem still sicker
  When they're taken down verbatim.

His motives may be miry,
  His priorities quite wrong,
But note this in your diary:
  He's the Singer, not the Song.

Forget the froth, the flannel -
  (It's really just for show).
Please see him as a channel
  Through which much Grace may flow.

Though his vestments may be glistening
  And his views on marriage wrong,
When his sermons make poor listening –
  Just remember, all along,

That the Song is Truth Eternal
  On which the Gospel stands;
And the Singer's just the one who puts
  The wafer in our hands.

Though his Patron be a belted earl
     Whose lineage is long,
And though he seems to you a churl
     Who's clearly in the wrong,
Do not forget that – in God's world
     When all is said and done -
The Vicar's just the Singer, not the Song!

July 2017

WHY HANG YOUR HEART ON THINGS ?

Why hang your heart on THINGS, my friend?
     What price the present pleasure?
These toys come soonest to an end –
     True worth is beyond measure.

Such boons are in Heaven's gift to send:
Rude health! Raw energy to spend!
The wit to know and apprehend
     The fruits of work and leisure!
Men's love on which you can depend!
The love of God, which has no end -
These gifts outweigh all else, my friend,
They are life's greatest dividend,
     Here is the real treasure!

November 2016

ST PETER

'It is a fact, from which we can take heart,
That greatness often comes from faulty start:

No start more faulty, nor no story sweeter
Than that of Simon - who became St Peter!

Peter, who left his Master in the lurch,
Became the Rock on which God built His Church!

His vows of deathless loyalty were not kept:
Small wonder that at cockcrow Peter wept!

This was the man who, in his pride complete,
Refused to let his Master wash his feet.

His fellow fishermen he durst outflank
By walking on the water – but he sank!

Uncouth – and yet on holy ground he trod:
"You are the true Son of the living God!"

Peter, whose faith and friendship were so flawed,
Was yet the first to see the risen Lord.

This fisherman, who quailed when tempest-tossed,
Preached fearless on the day of Pentecost!

Though to a servant-girl he cowardly lied.
The mighty Sanhedrin he yet defied!

The man who once forsook Christ, to his shame,
Evangelised the Gentiles in Christ's Name!

A martyr, he, who – seeing how Christ died –
Himself (they say) was likewise crucified.

Though once of cowards deemed the very worst,
Among the Twelve Apostles he is first!

He who escaped from gaol, angel-driven,
Is now the Keeper of the Keys of Heaven!

Peter's repentance brought its own reward –
Divine forgiveness, fellowship restored.
Likewise may all men know the risen Lord!

May 2017
St Peter's, Rome

IN MY FATHER'S HOUSE...

St John 14:2 *"In my Father's house are many mansions…*
I go to prepare a place for you."

I should not be afraid to die,
    New scenes I will embrace ;
This world is good - but by and by
    I'll find a better place.

I'll need (my present house outgrown)
    A change of domicile,
An upgrade to the stately home
    Which waits for me the while.

A smooth transition I foresee,
    A house-move without stress,
And 'Many Mansions' then will be
    My permanent address.

I shall not take my things with me,
    Possessions are mere clutter;
My lifestyle will more lavish be
    Than ever tongue could utter.

Though certainty is what I crave
    And doubt more than I should,
Whatever lies beyond the grave
    I do believe is good!

April 2015

PLANS

Rashly short-sighted we were born,
    Folly all ages spans!
In case tomorrow may not dawn,
    Sit lightly to your plans.

"Eat, drink, be merry!" some have said,
    "Let power and pleasure rule!"
Boldly the Rich Man planned ahead –
    God said to him: "You fool!"

So if you want to make God laugh
    Just tell Him all your plans.
Your tomb will bear this epitaph:
    "Our times are in HIS hands."

June 2012 ✍

O PLACE OF PEACE, JERUSALEM

I compose music for the piano as well as choral music for use in worship. This hymn was composed as per instructions for a 'Writer News' competition, to be sung to the tune of 'O Little Town of Bethlehem' (Forest Green) - July 1997

O place of peace, Jerusalem,
    Set high on Zion's hill,
Where, crucified, our Saviour died,
    God's purpose to fulfil;
And where He left an empty tomb
    We come His Name to bless,
While pilgrims throng its streets along –
    A place of holiness.

O David's royal Jerusalem
    Where still the Temple wall
Proclaims its hour of erstwhile power,
    Its ancient rise and fall,
Where Christ, rejected and despis'd
    Received not by His own,
So low did lie - but mounted high,
    Ascended to His throne.

Jerusalem, Jerusalem,
    Your prophets you have slain!
Your house was left, destroy'd, bereft,
    Today you stand again!
We see a city shining
    Where God's great love was shown,
His diadem, Jerusalem,
    And Christ its cornerstone.

THE SECOND COMING

It happened late one evening, in a manner I had not expected –
Unannounced, without clamour,
Without the smallest signal of its cataclysmic nature.
My parents were out, their return inexplicably delayed.
Desperation grew.

Suddenly, alone in the house, I knew that I had been left behind,
That the world had changed for ever,
That the unnoticed God had stepped in and taken
                              everything away,
Or rather, had taken away those things most immediate
                              to me, my parents -
Caught up, it was certain, in a flaming chariot of joy
Along with all the believers.
I was left behind. The Second Coming had come and gone.
The sheep and goats had been sorted.

I had read "The one shall be taken, the other left"
And had not wholly believed, thinking it a threat too far.
But now I knew – beyond peradventure – that it was true,
That the day of the Lord had come "like a thief in the night".
And I knew at that moment the totality of my exclusion.
Too young to understand fully the language of eschatology
And yet old enough to be familiar with its images,
I looked into the abyss and saw my own damnation.

And then – thank God! – my parents returned, unaware
        of any Divine intervention.
Relief was unconfined.
Since that day I have known that the Second Coming
        is yet to be.

October 2014

TRUTH

"What is truth?' said jesting Pilate and would not stay for an answer." - Bacon

O tell me the truth about beauty,
    Such beauty as haunts us from youth.
To know it, said Keats, is our duty,
    'Gainst ageing and death it is proof.
Inscrutable claim: "Truth is Beauty – *
    All we need to know – Beauty is Truth"!

O tell me the truth about passion,
    Such passions as all men torment,
The pain of denied satisfaction,
    The pangs of divine discontent
Which, after despair or elation,
    Leave us "calm of mind, all passion spent".*

O tell me the truth about loving,
    Such love as the poets extol,
The love that is healing, illuming,
    Without which no creature is whole.
And all we achieve is worth nothing
    If we love not – both body and soul.

O tell me the truth about living
    And whether this lifetime is all
And whether – rejoicing or grieving –
    There's anything lasts at all
And whether eternal Forgiving
    Awaits us when, groping, we fall.

"What is truth?" Pontius Pilate said, jesting,
  And would not stay for reply,
With half-truths content to be resting,
  Lest found to be living a lie.
Dear God! May I never cease questing
  To know what is true – or I die!

Cape Town, November 2015

*Keats: Ode to a Grecian Urn
*Milton: 'Samson Agonistes'

THE CROSS

The cross was where men chose to chasten God.
The hands that kindly healed, the feet that trod
The Galilean waters – these they nailed,
Hammered through splintering bone, and spat and railed
And laughed, while money for his clothes they gave:
"He saved others; himself he cannot save!"

Then earthquakes came, and darkness, and he cried
"God, why have you forsaken me?" – and died.
A lone centurion knelt in holy dread
Before that hanging Jew and bowed his head:
"Truly this was the Son of God!" he said.

March 2015

THE RESURRECTION

"It cannot be," in disbelief they said -
Those who had claimed none rises from the dead.
The woman, seeing a gardener close at hand,
Spoke, weeping, for she did not understand:
The corpse was gone, small wonder she was wary! –
Until that moment and that one word "Mary".

The same day, disillusionment and chaos
Clouded the minds of walkers to Emmaus –
Until that moment when the bread was blessed
At table by their unsuspected Guest.
How strange that closest friends could misconstrue Him!
But now their eyes were opened and they knew Him.

How could those fishermen at sea forget
His features when He told them "Cast the net"? -
No recognition, not a sign to snatch –
Until that moment of a record catch.
Astonishment! So many fish aboard! -
"Who art thou?" Then they knew it was the Lord.

The evidence of others Thomas flouted.
Because he could not touch the wounds, he doubted -
Until that moment when, through the shut door,
Came Jesus in the flesh, just as before.
Much mortified, the truth he now perceived:
"My Lord and God" said Thomas – and believed!

Which goes to show, whatever our objection,
It doesn't do to doubt the Resurrection!

March 2015

THE MAGI

"What is this strange new star," we said,
    "Which last night crossed the sky?
Tonight it shines again – and stands
    Quite motionless on high
As if to pour its light upon
    Some miracle nearby."

"Why does that star stand still?" we asked,
    "While all else spins around?
Alone it casts a steady light
    Where flickering ones abound,
As though directing us to seek
    Some piece of holy ground.

"See how it goes ahead " we cried,
    "Now that we follow near!
The many stars it does not heed,
    It moves in its own sphere!
And now – oh look! - it moves no more.
    Why has it stopped just here?"

'Tis for a King (some wise men say)
    That we have come so far –
A King that you will find (they say)
    Beneath a guiding star,
A King that's over and above
    All other Kings that are.

A King, they say, whom men will kill,
    Whose garments will be sold,
Whose suffering and humbling are
    His destiny foretold.
Our gifts must be, most fittingly,
    Myrrh, frankincense and gold.

We did not comfortably come,
    Our quest was not for ease.
We leave behind the worldly mind,
    The passing things that please.
Our search is done. To this young Child
    We fall upon our knees.

May 2013

199

LIVE EACH DAY AS IF IT
'TWERE THY LAST

God knows which day! The die is cast!
    Years fly away,
    Our time goes fast -
Then live each day as 'twere thy last!

It profits not to rue the past:
    It's now diminished,
    Done and finished,
So live each day as 'twere thy last.

'Tis well, whether at feast or fast,
    At work or rest,
    Relaxed or stressed,
To live each day as 'twere thy last.

The sun may bless, the storm may blast –
    The clouds may burst,
    Wind blows its worst -
But live each day as 'twere thy last.

Each dawn brings treasures unsurpassed,
    Such truths are found
    As break new ground,
So live each day as 'twere thy last!

And every hour shows prospects vast
    - From windows wide -
    Of tracks untried.
Then live each day as 'twere thy last.

(If such a thought leaves thee aghast
And fearful as the day goes past -
Take heart! It may NOT be thy last!)

August 2017

TO MY FATHER

To my father, terminally ill, Easter 1977. (He died of cancer in September)

As God's mercy is made known
In the midst of pain and loss
And His lovingkindness shown
In the starkness of the cross –
So may YOU know His comradeship
As Easter flowers bloom
And feast upon His fellowship
Beside the empty tomb!

*George Eric Hunt on a
family holiday, Polzeath,
North Cornwall 1971*

SAINT MARK

"And there followed [Jesus] a certain
young man having a linen cloth cast about
his naked body, and the young men laid
hold on him – and he left the linen cloth
and fled from them naked." (St Mark 14: 51,52)
(It is usually assumed that the young man
was St Mark himself.)

When faith is shaken, love betrayed
    And hope is all but dead,
Your nakedness is ours, too,
    As on the day you fled
And in your flight your self-belief
    And garments all were shed.

Yet you brought God to Africa!
    Your martyrdom atones -
That cruel dragging through the streets,
    That shredding on the stones.
And then to Venice, relics sweet,
    They took your sacred bones.

Your Gospel tells a story
    Of humility and love,
Of One on whom the Holy Ghost
    Descended like a dove,
And who, obedient unto death,
    Arose and reigns above.

And servant-hood is all your theme:
　　The Servant self-confessed
Came not to BE served but to serve,
　　His role made manifest
All mother-naked on the Cross
　　But now in glory dressed.

Venetian grandeur may compel
　　A visitor to stare
And Mark's Basilica may well
　　Soar high above the Square
And lovelier than words can tell
　　Is Venice, rich and rare.
Yet 'tis that young man's nakedness
(His helplessness, his faithlessness)
　　Which summons us to prayer.

March 2017

THINGS ECCLESIASTICAL

(With apologies to the Walrus and the Carpenter)

A friend of ours, who happens to be a bishop, invited his small circle of poetry lovers to find (or compose) a poem with this title. This was my contribution. No individual bishop is targeted! The nonsense may, or may not, be making a serious point.

"The time has come" the Bishop said
    To talk of the fantastical,
To deal, all inhibitions shed,
    With things ecclesiastical
And whether now the way ahead
    Should be iconoclastical.

"It is high time" the Bishop said
    To talk of weighty things:
Of how the Catholics are misled
    And whether Methodism's dead
And what if angels are cross-bred
    And whether saints have wings.

"The time is ripe" the Bishop cried
    "To make the Church more happy,
To rid us of the starry-eyed
And churchmanship we can't abide –
High Church, with incense on the side
    And Low Church happy-clappy."

The Bishop said "Discuss we must
    Transubstantiation
And what should be the Church's thrust,
Considering that all flesh is dust -
And is it, therefore, right to trust
    To one's imagination?

And whether, when we eastward face,
    We bow in meek subjection –
Or whether there's a stronger case
    For prostrate genuflection?"
The Bishop said (a wise man, he)
    "Denying it seems heretical –
But on the other hand, you see,
    The problem's hypothetical –
It doesn't pay to bow the knee,
(Indeed, it can most painful be),
    The benefits are theoretical."

He said "My crook, my pectoral cross,
    My episcopal regalia –
Although, of course, I call them dross,
I fear I would be at a loss
    Without pontificalia.
    My God! I'd feel a failure."

"Prayer books" he said, "come fast and thick
    In versions old and new:
Ancient or modern – take your pick!
(Of good ones there are few.}
As for myself, I think I'll stick
    To 1662." ☛

The Bishop said "'Tis time to tweet
About all problems clerical :
How should an Anglo-Catholic greet
(If he should meet one in the street)
     A twice-born Evangelical?"

Said he "Although I'm no fanatic,
Some of my flock, being charismatic,
     Are prone to stretch their lungs:
They have a way of being dramatic
And disconcertingly ecstatic,
     Speaking in foreign tongues."

The Bishop said "The time has come
     To examine every miracle -
And whether, as a rule of thumb,
To scepticism we succumb:
     Our approach must be empirical."
The Bishop said "A man sincere
     I've no wish to disparage.
On women bishops I'm not clear;
Just as ambivalent appear
     My views on same-sex marriage."

The Bishop said "I've no desire
     That men should think me cynical:
Clearly the Church should now aspire
     To be more ecumenical –
So long as this does not backfire
Or mortally offend the Squire:
     We must appear canonical."
He further spoke: "I am inclined

206

To think God's allegorical!
Is He a figment of the mind?
Are all believers simply blind?
    Is the Devil SO diabolical?

"Talking of hats," he said, "Heigh-ho!
    I have a gorgeous mitre!
Such headgear makes a splendid show,
    The Church is all the brighter!
(A biretta might be better, though,
    Also a little lighter.)"

The Bishop sighed "Time's running out,
    The Church is going to pot!
The fabric's crumbling, have no doubt!
With church finances up the spout
We'll have to learn to do without -
    I fear my bolt is shot."

"The time is up" the Bishop wailed,
    "Our work has scarce begun.
Why is it that the Church has failed?" -
    But answer came there none.
The congregation, long downscaled,
    Had vanished, every one!

August 2015 ✍

Ancient Gargoyle from
Cartmel Priory, Cumbria

THIS WAY UP

September 2017

*(A poem occasioned by seeing an upside-down
box with this instruction writ large on it.)*

"THIS WAY UP" the package said,
Its message: "Not, please, on my head
Or (just as risky) on my side -
Positions I cannot abide.
Please leave me standing right side up"
- To no avail! The game was up!
A box may split, or spill, or leak
Or, under pressure, crack and break
Or hold, perhaps, a brimming cup:
Best leave it standing this way up!
Its contents may well be alive,
Which, upside down, will not survive -
A cherished cat, a precious pup,
A lovesome lamb, a lustful tup!
In which case, keep it this way up!

Lifelong we voyage in a box,
Floating like jetsam near the rocks
And, gasping like a stranded scup,
We suffer, being the wrong way up.
Thus through our drifting days we strive
To be upright – and so survive.
We hope, the world being upside down,
Being right side up we will not drown.
All equilibrium is lost:
We are at sea and tempest-tossed
And, while on horrors we may sup,
The tilting world (our brimming cup) ❖